CONTENTS

Introduction 1

Chapter 1. Build your credibility 6

How you can build positive influence through personal credibility.

Chapter 2. Tip the ratio 55

How to build the positive to negative ratio when interacting with others.

Chapter 3. Project warmth 65

How you can increase your level of warmth and encouragement with others.

Chapter 4. Empower others 90

Different types of power and how we can use them, abuse them and let go of them.

Chapter 5. Establish clear boundaries 109

How to become more assertive, give feedback and manage conflict.

Positive Influence

Harnessing the Power of Positive Psychology to build effective relationships

Peter Connolly

Copyright © 2013 Peter Connolly

All rights reserved.

ISBN-13:
978-1492162667

ISBN-10:
1492162663

Chapter 6. Manage your firewall 153

How to raise awareness of personal filters and barriers to good communication and deeper relationships.

Chapter 7. Value differences 162

Focuses on how to understand, appreciate and facilitate different personalities, strengths and motivations in self and others.

Chapter 8. Transcending & leading the way 198

Focuses on how we can choose to act as leaders and positive role models regardless of the context.

Chapter 9. The Whole Symphony 213

Looking at the bigger picture.

Appendix 217

64 ways to improve your positive influence

ACKNOWLEDGMENTS

Special thanks to Inez, Jimmy, Sarah and Derek all of whom helped to make this book more readable.

Dedicated to Sarah, the strongest person I know and the most positive influence on my life.

Introduction

"It is important that students bring a certain ragamuffin, barefoot irreverence to their studies; they are not here to worship what is known, but to question it."

Jacob Bronowski

"Few will have the greatness to bend history itself, but each of us can work to change a small portion of events. It is from numberless diverse acts of courage and belief that human history is shaped. Each time a man stands up for an ideal, or acts to improve the lot of others, or strikes out against injustice, he sends forth a tiny ripple of hope……. "

Robert F. Kennedy

"We delight in the beauty of the butterfly, but rarely admit the changes it has gone through to achieve that beauty."

Maya Angelou

About Influence and influencing

We are, each and everyone one of us, influencing in just about every interaction we have, whether it is a casual acquaintance, a customer, a manager, a work team, a family member, a child, a politician or any other person or group of people with whom we come into contact.

In these interactions we are usually either having a neutral, negative or positive influence.

Being highly intelligent creatures that have achieved a significant level of self-awareness we are capable of adapting our behaviour so as to potentially vary the kind of influence we have. This book provides a number of concepts, ideas and practical methods to help you raise your awareness of your current approach to influencing and adapt it skillfully so as to achieve a higher level of positive influence.

Reading with purpose.

At the time of writing this book I have two school age children to whom I offer help when they need it (and probably too often when they don't). My eldest son will sometimes take time to study by himself. Occasionally I will chat with him afterwards and ask him some questions about what he has studied. In the early stages when I did this he would often remember nothing at all. This reminded me of some of my own experiences when studying for my undergraduate degree. I would come back to a book I had read which would be covered in highlighter pen, yet it was, to me, as if I had never read it before. I eventually got into the habit of actively reading and studying so that when it came to studying for my post graduate degree I would spend less time studying but remembering significantly more of what I needed. I am also trying to help my two children to see the benefit in this habit. Whether I succeed could be somewhat dependent on how clever I am at applying some of the concepts in this book. If you are reading this in about 2020 feel free to check with me on how successful I was – assuming I am still around.

I recommend that you read this book as actively as possible. The likelihood of it being of any use is a lot greater if you do.

Firstly, consider your COGs: this stands for challenges, opportunities and goals.

Challenges

What challenges do you currently face in relation to influencing or bringing out the best in others?

Opportunities:

What opportunities do you have to practice what you will learn in this book? Identify two or three people that you will focus on while reading and practicing.

Goals:

What are your goals in relation to what you will learn in this book? If you were to improve in your ability to influence what would that give you?

As well as doing the above I suggest you do as many of the exercises in the book as possible and that you take notes while reading.

Lastly I do not profess to be a brilliant practitioner of everything in this book. I have bad days and good days and even people who probably "hate my stinking guts" as the kid used to say in the "Little Rascals". However, I will say that I do the best I can to be as positive an influence as I can be while at the same time falling foul of my own ego, arrogance, and human frailties from time to time.

Chapter 1

Build Your Credibility

cred·i·bil·i·ty; the quality or power of inspiring belief. The quality of being trusted.

"Your beliefs become your thoughts,
Your thoughts become your words,
Your words become your actions,
Your actions become your habits,
Your habits become your values,
Your values become your destiny."

M.K. Gandhi

"if one advances confidently in the direction of his dreams, and endeavours to live the life which he has imagined, he will meet with a success unexpected in common hours."

Henry David Thoreau

Do people believe in you? Do they place their trust in you? Would they describe you as reliable? Do they see you as a person who has the courage to state what you believe in and to act accordingly? Are you competent in your area of speciality? This chapter is about answering these questions and a little more besides.

It is very difficult to bring out the best in others if they neither trust nor believe in you nor if they cannot see what your intentions are. Jim Kouzes and Barry Posner in their research for their book The Leadership Challenge repeatedly have found that honesty is the most important quality that people look for in a leader they would willingly follow. They saw this as so crucial as to justify a book specifically devoted to credibility.

Over the last decade or so I have been carrying out a piece of informal research during workshops that focuses on trust and credibility. Part of this research involves a short exercise which you can carry out yourself.

I ask the group to think of a colleague or manager in whom they have very little trust. I then ask them to capture on a sticky note some of the behaviours that have demonstrated to them that this colleague cannot be trusted. I then gather up all of the sticky notes from the participants and place them on a flipchart or pin-board. Following this I repeat the process but this time asking them to think of someone in whom they have a high level of trust and once again place the sticky notes on the flipchart. I have done this with literally thousands of people and the same kinds of qualities and behaviours come up repeatedly. Some of these qualities are shown below.

Examples of qualities that were believed to reduce trust:

"Talked about me behind my back"

"Broke promises"

"Didn't listen or pay attention"

"Was dishonest"

"Never encouraged me"

"Said one thing did another"

Examples of qualities that were believed to increase trust:

"Kept promises"

"Had clear intentions and expectations"

"Encouraged or supported others"

"Honesty"

"Gave credit where credit was due"

"Walked his/her talk"

Based on this research as well as a ten year meta-analysis of the research and theories of others I have developed a model for credibility. I believe that using the model to understand your current level of credibility is a good starting point for personal self-awareness. If you take the time to do the exercises included in this chapter the model will also help you to increase your influence and trust with others and over time will help you to transcend petty issues, build character and inspire confidence in yourself and others.

Aristotle described three levels of influence in his Treatise on Rhetoric. At the surface we influence through logos or the appeal to logic we make when communicating. The next level down is pathos, the way we relate to others emotionally or how well we empathise with others. The deepest level is ethos, who we are at our core, our ethical ground or our character. I have used an expanded version of this concept for my model of credibility. Before going through the model in detail you might like to take the credibility review which is at the end of this chapter.

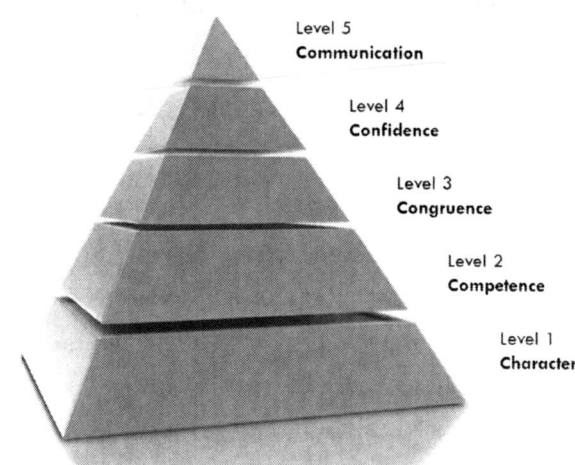

The Credibility Pyramid

Credibility Level 1. Character

The foundation of the model is character. In the context of this model character means how you express your internal values and how others perceive you over time. It is often interpreted as meaning how well you walk your talk.

When it comes to character there are three main principles.

The first is that you know what you value and what values drive your behaviour. I do not mean a theoretical exercise in stating your values but a genuine attempt at knowing and living what really matters most to you.

As Stephen Covey puts it,

How different our lives are when we really know what is deeply important to us, and, keeping that picture in mind, we manage ourselves each day to be and to do what matters most. - Stephen Covey, The 7 Habits of Highly Effective People

The challenge at this level of the pyramid is that often people say they value one thing but act as if they value something quite different.

For example a manager states that she values a good balance between work and personal life but she constantly stays late, comes in on Saturdays and rarely takes time to herself.

The second principle of character is that you are clear about what your intentions are in regard to self and others.

People want to know what your intended behaviour is. Clear intentions make it easier to trust you and to feel safe in your company and where trust is higher things tend to happen easier and faster. I have often heard the comment, "I would prefer a tough honest manager who tells it like it is as opposed to a 'nicer', more passive manager who keeps his or her cards close to his or her chest." With the tough honest manager at least we know what to expect and when we know what to expect we can plan or act accordingly.

Whether it's getting a clear vision for the next ten years or clarifying our needs in a difficult conversation, defining and communicating a clear sense of intention or vision is, in my opinion, essential to building character.

Kouzes and Posner put it very simply when they write,

"It's the ability to imagine or discover a desirable destination toward which the company, agency, congregation or community should head."

And according to Peter Senge et al,

Genuine visions arise from crystallizing a larger intent..... - Peter Senge et al, Presence

A very simple example of the communication of clear intention often occurs when walking down a crowded street. Sometimes when we walk straight towards a person we enter into a kind of dance where each person keeps going to go around but ends up moving in the same direction as the other. You will find that if you walk down a crowded street with your eyes focused on something specific in the distance that this will rarely ever happen, this is because your intention is clear from the look on your face and from your body language and the other person knows which way to walk based on the signals you are giving off. If only we could keep our intentions this clear most of the time, people would find us much easier to trust because they would know what to expect from us. Unfortunately we too often keep our intentions hidden and we enter into a similar psychological dance when confronted with others.

For some reason we often learn from an early age that it is better to keep our intentions hidden. This is often because we fear offending or hurting others. Many of us learn a form of over-responsibility for others, from an early age, we internalise messages that tell us we should take care not to hurt others with our feelings and our intentions. This often leads to us not being open with others, having false intentions, feeling like we have to take care of others and not being assertive. The irony is that our lack of courage to communicate who we truly are often causes more harm than we realise.

Without clear intention it is often as if we are driving in fog. However at least when driving in fog we usually know what our desired destination is.

The third principle is that you do what you say you will do; you act in accordance with your values and intentions.

There is an experience I have had that most of us seem to have at some stage. I am at home, downstairs and I think to myself, "I left my watch upstairs in the bedroom, I must go up and get it." I am halfway up the stairs and someone calls to me, "are you going upstairs could you bring me down my ipod," (cardigan, keys, wallet or a multitude of other things). I go on upstairs and I get the ipod or whatever for the person who asked for it. I then either go back down stairs having forgotten my watch or I pause up there and wonder what I came up for in the first place.

If I had consciously kept both things (valuing both) at the front of my mind I could easily have remembered the two but instead one stepped in and replaced the other.

This reminds me of the relationship we often have with our deeper values or sense of purpose; we do not keep them at the forefront of our minds and they get shunted for other things. I am not saying those other things are more or less important than our values. However, it is very difficult to be true to our values or stay connected with our purpose if we,

1. are not clear of what they are.

2. keep them somewhere in the back of our

minds.

3. allow other more immediate thinks slip in and shunt them all the time.

I believe that if we keep our values and our guiding purpose and intentions clear and at the front of our minds they will help us to make more beneficial short and long term decisions. We can even choose when it may be necessary to set them aside so as to put others first. Clear values and clear intentions help you to realise how you, ultimately, can best add value to the lives of others.

When people see you follow through on commitments they receive affirmation that you are who you say you are. The more they see this, the more they observe your character in action and feel they can believe in you.

Exercise: Do you truly know what you value? How can you discern what your true values are?

Try to identify what you value and prioritize in regard to the following,

- Personal health - physical and psychological.
- Your family and friends.
- Work colleagues.
- Money and finance
- Other values (politics, art, holidays etc.)

Now go to some of the people affected by the above and ask them if they agree that your behaviour demonstrates that you truly value what you say you do. Ask them to be as honest as they can be. This can provide valuable feedback in regard to your character and what it is like to be on the receiving end of you as a person.

Exercise: To get into the habit of aligning your behaviour with your values at the beginning of each day ask yourself,

"What will I do today to show that I cherish my values?"

And at the end of each day ask yourself.

"What did I do today that showed that I cherish my values?"

Then ask yourself how you need to alter your behaviour so as to keep your focus true.

Exercise. To explore your character further take some time to answer the questions below.

Imagine yourself looking down from above at you in your current situation. What is important to you about what you are focusing on and doing at the moment?

Ultimately what is it that you are trying to achieve or influence?

How would you describe your ideal approach to influencing others?

In ten to twenty years what would you like your close friends, close colleagues or close family members to say about you and the influence you had on them?

Credibility level 2: Competence

The second level of credibility, competence, is to do with your knowledge, skill and expertise in your specific domain in whatever context you are considering at the time.

If you are being operated on by a surgeon you want their competence to be high. If you are being flown somewhere in an aeroplane you would most likely prefer the pilot to have all of the requisite knowledge needed to fly the plane effectively. If, however, we discover that competence is lacking in either of these situations we may find ourselves feeling a little nervous. Other people's competence usually means they are secure and confident in their abilities and hence contributes to bringing out the best in us. Therefore if we achieve competence in our own area of expertise we too are likely to bring out the best in others. People find it easier to follow someone who knows what they are doing.

Exercise: Consider the following,

How knowledgeable are you in your areas of focus on a scale of 1 to 10 where 10 is expert or role model?

How effective and skilful are you, also on a scale of 1 to 10 where ten is expert?

If you scored yourself below a 10 in the above assessment what do you need to do to improve your score by just one point? What reading, teaching, training or practicing do you need to start doing to improve your perceived score? It could also be useful to ask others to score you.

One of the ways that we can significantly damage our credibility is to claim competence where it is not present. Some people hate to appear ignorant or incompetent and so they give an air of competence despite the fact that competence is actually lacking. I can sometimes fall into this category myself and I have learned the hard way that it is much better for all concerned to admit ones ignorance and be willing to say, "I don't know" when appropriate. In the long run people usually prefer honesty to pretence.

Credibility level 3. Congruence

Congruence can be one of the most difficult levels of the pyramid to achieve but I believe it is the quality that bridges and aligns all of the levels. I came across the concept of congruence first when I studied the work of Carl Rogers who had a significant influence on the world of counselling and psychotherapy.

Rogers' work led him to conclude that there are three fundamental conditions required for personal growth to take place in any therapeutic relationship. These conditions are,

1. Unconditional positive regard – having a sense of regard that is not dependent on the other person being or doing anything.

2. Empathy – Being able to get a felt sense of what another is thinking and feeling and being able to communicate that sense to the person.

3. Congruence – The ability to express the self that one truly is. Being genuine and true to who you really are.

According to Carl Rogers congruence,

"means that within the relationship he (sic) is freely and deeply himself, with his actual experience represented by his awareness of himself. It is the opposite of presenting a façade…"

It was the quality of congruence that Rogers found to be the most difficult to achieve and he wrote of this right up to the time just before he died.

Congruence is essentially achieving an alignment between what you communicate, what you believe, what you need, what you value and how you feel in a particular moment. The person who achieves congruence comes across as natural. If they give an impression of positivity you find that this is genuine not something they are putting on for show. They are comfortable in their own skin and in what they are doing. You get a sense from them that they are attempting to or doing what they love and are good at. Because of this they find it easy to be quietly confident and to assert themselves when necessary. They will be clear about who they are and what really matters to them and they will have found or be in the process of finding a path that is meaningful to them. This rootedness in what is important to them and focus on their personal strengths tends to give them a sense of security and stability that serves to guide them in most situations. As a result the person who achieves congruence will often find it easier to listen empathically to others. They are not threatened by the darker areas that true empathy can give voice to. Real listening requires that we enter the unknown world of the other and to do this requires that the listener have a good personal lighthouse to guide them.

When we achieve congruence we are also more likely to listen to ourselves, our inner needs and motivations and we are likely to take responsibility for ourselves. That is, we admit to our faults without making excuses or over explaining why we behave the way we do.

Generally I think congruence is an indication of a level of maturity wherein one has begun to accept one's humanness. We become accepting of the fact that we are not perfect, we make mistakes, we need help and we know less than we once thought we did. Although, I do not profess to having achieved this, often I *do* think that the closer I get to it the more I tend to feel both vulnerable and confident at the same time. That paradox I don't yet fully understand but I hope to maybe cover it in a later book when I am either wiser or dumber than I am now.

Exercise: Over the coming days become aware of specific times when you feel like your values, needs, intentions and feelings are in alignment with what you are expressing through language or behaviour. Notice how you feel at that time. Notice the impact you are having with others.

Then become aware of when there is misalignment between your values, needs, intentions, feelings and self expression. Ask yourself where you think the incongruence lies. Try to reflect on your experience and establish what you would need to do to be more true to yourself in that moment . Ask yourself what, specifically, you would have expressed if you had been more true to your self. If you believe you should have said something different try saying the words and see if they feel more genuine.

Credibility Level 4 – Confidence

Confidence is our belief in our-selves and our ability to act in and interact with the world. When we are confident we hold a picture of ourselves in our mind that is relatively close to what and who we really are.

Real confidence is not arrogance. There is no need to brag. We are just willing to admit that we are good at some things and not so good at others. There is a strong connection between confidence, competence and character. While others can help us to feel confident and our environment can shake our confidence, true confidence is a quality that comes from within; it stems from a sense of knowing ones strengths, capacities, values and vision.

When we are highly confident we trust that regardless of what happens we have the capacity to plan and achieve goals and to adapt to our environment. I call this kind of confidence, **root confidence.** It is rooted from within and not dependent on what we have to weather externally.

If we are sailing a ship we are, to some extent, dependent on many things to feel confident in our capacity to complete our journey. Our confidence in the ship stems from the integrity of its design and build. Our confidence in the guidance systems stems from their accuracy. Our confidence in the crew stems from our experience with them and our confidence in our journey is dependent to some extent on the maps we use.

However, if we find ourselves caught in a storm that sends us off course and damages the instruments and other equipment what do we have to fall back on? It is at these times that we require root confidence, a faith in our character, that its integrity will remain intact. In such times we need to draw from within to help us navigate through the current storm. Some people learn this at an early age, or they are placed in circumstances that teach them this lesson. Others have to learn it when they are older and some may never learn it. Instead, for whatever reason, they never get a chance to rise above being a victim of circumstance.

It is my firm belief that knowing our strengths and values and being clear about what matters most to us will contribute significantly to our feeling strong in times of crisis. If we are caught in a burning building and a fire-fighter finds us and tells us that they are going to guide us out and that we will be okay we are likely to place our trust in this person. Why? Because they know what they are doing and they know what the primary goal is in that moment. Imagine what your reaction might be if that same fire-fighter came to you and said, *"This is crazy. The building's on fire, I'm not sure if we are going to make it out of here, there are so many things to do I am not sure which one I should do first."* The fire-fighter knows that even though he or she may feel fear, trepidation and discomfort what is required is a confident approach. As Brian Tracy would say we need to have "confident expectations".

To some extent people who have congruence between their character and competence are likely to automatically have a fairly strong sense of confidence. However, because we all have our innate temperament and a certain amount of baggage we can still be lacking in self-belief; despite knowing what we know about ourselves we may have adopted inner voices that tend to darken or warp our image of who we truly are.

One of the most common discussions I have had with clients in coaching and in counselling is that they feel they may some-day be found out for who they really are.

Developing confidence

The fact is that when people show a genuine confidence in themselves they are more likely to influence others to feel comfortable and confident.

There are many different kinds of confidence but for the purposes of this book I will divide confidence into three types,

1. Environmentally induced confidence.

2. Present moment inner confidence.

3. Root confidence.

Environmentally induced confidence is external to us whereas the other two are internal sources of confidence. Environmentally induced confidence comes from reading the expiry date of a food item and seeing that it is in date or putting on the handbrake and feeling the car holding. There is little we can do in most of these circumstances but they do inspire confidence.

You can improve present moment inner confidence in a number of different ways such as:

Visualizing a positive state

Positive self-talk,

Building positive associations with a state you wish to create,

Adjusting your posture,

Deep breathing techniques.

I also believe that practices such as yoga, tai chi, good exercise routines, meditation, martial arts and others can contribute to improving present moment confidence.

The other thing that can improve present moment confidence is practicing whatever it is we are required to do, for example, practising presentations continually tends to lead to increased confidence in this area. This of course shows further the integration between the layers of the credibility model, where competence and confidence tend to dynamically interact.

Root Confidence

You can improve deep rooted confidence in different ways but this generally takes longer.

There are typically two broad approaches, one is containing and reducing recurring self-confidence detractors and the second is by building your connection to your inner source of strength.

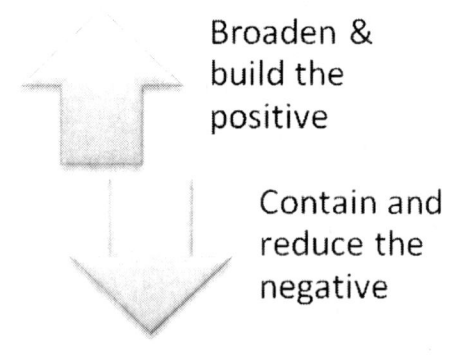

Broaden & build the positive

Contain and reduce the negative

Self-confidence detractors are pieces of baggage that impact on your sense of who you really are. They are often old voices, thoughts, feelings, reactions and mental maps that were laid down in the past. We typically create these in our formative years as a way of responding to the world and fitting in with it. For example I was told by a teacher when I was 12 that I was "a sneaky little shit". I remember how these words reverberated in my mind for a long time afterward. I think what made it significant, because I had certainly heard worse from friends and peers, was that I respected this particular teacher. Regardless, I took that message in and for a long time afterwards believed this is how people saw me. Most of us have many different experiences like this. The challenge is that we often use these messages as the brushes to paint the internal picture of who we are.

The ABC model from cognitive behavioural therapy can help with these detractors. A. stands for Adversary or activating event and C. stands for consequence. The challenge most of us face is that we skip the B stage and go straight from A to C. For example you tell me you don't like my hair – I think you have made me sad, annoyed, irritated. Or my boss doesn't praise my presentation – I think he has made me feel lousy, undermined, unconfident. In each example I have left out the B part which is the Belief or attitude or internal rule in my mind that allows the activating event to have control over me. I am obviously in need of being told my hair looks well or my presentation went well and if I don't get these external affirmations I feel some negative emotion.

Sometimes these reactions are very well programmed in our unconscious and they happen so quickly that it is hard to gain control over them. However, if we can begin to raise our awareness of the internal beliefs and rules that lead us into negative states we can begin to gain some power over them. Hence either containing them, reducing them, replacing them or removing them altogether.

The best practice that I have come across for raising awareness of some of these reactions and containing and reducing the negative is the one I learned at a Buddhist workshop I attended. What this involves seems simple. However, when you attempt it for the first time in the middle of a difficult feeling or event you realise it is more difficult than you would imagine.

Exercise: Containing and reducing negative emotions,

Pick something you still feel bitter or angry about.

Start by allowing yourself to become aware of whatever arises – thoughts, feelings, physical discomfort, judgement etc.

As you become more aware of what is going on notice whether you accept what arises.

Then say to yourself, " breathing in I am aware of .... (anger, for example) arising in me, breathing out I am letting go of ...."(you may not be letting go of the anger but you are letting go of the breath). Try doing this three to five times.

Exercise: Broaden and Build the Positive

Bring to mind a time when you felt good about yourself. It can be from childhood, the teen years, early adulthood or within the last few months. Try to remember it in as much detail as possible: where you were, what you were doing, what you were wearing, who else was there, what you thought and felt at the time. Whatever the feeling was bring it back to mind and body now. As you remember this think of a word or sentence that best describes or labels this memory then press your thumb against your forefinger. As you press your thumb and forefinger try to make the memory more vivid in your mind. Imagine the colours getting stronger, the feelings getting stronger. Try to remember it as if it only happened yesterday.

Practice bringing this memory back a few times over today and the next few days by pressing your thumb and forefinger together.

You will probably notice that when you engage fully with this exercise and genuinely remember a specific time that you experience a little lift in mood. Research has shown that remembering pleasant experiences can have a positive effect on our neurochemistry.

Once you have done this for one finger you can

easily go ahead and remember a positive trigger for each of the other three fingers. Then when you need to you can touch thumb to forefinger, middle finger, ring finger and pinkie and trigger a series of positive memories. If practiced, this exercise can work well for elevating mood and putting you in a more positive mind-state.

To really build root confidence, however, we need to get really clear about what drives us, what our life's purpose is, what matters to us so much that we would almost sacrifice anything to preserve it or give it life.

Few of us ever get that clear about mission or purpose but when you meet people who have, their confidence is usually quite notable. Their conviction and commitment to a cause or purpose gives them an inner strength that surpasses the context or the moment. One imagines that it is this kind of confidence that has given people like Gandhi the strength to go on hunger strike for human and Indian rights in India, Aung San Suu Kyi the strength to tolerate a decade and a half of house arrest in

Myanmar and Nelson Mandella the determination to never give up on the possibility of freedom from imprisonment and the apartheid regime in South Africa.

Credibility Level 5 Communication

Communication skill is primarily about two things: Firstly how we let others know our feelings, thoughts, opinions and intentions and secondly how we tune in to and respond to the feelings, thoughts, opinions and intentions of others.

We could summarise the mind-set, attitude and behaviours as either "letting out" or "letting in". "Letting out" being what we express through our body language and our words and "letting in" being when we are listening, attending and attempting to understand others. This is usually through silence, listening, attuning, clarifying etc.

"Letting Out"

When "letting out" the more that our communication is open and honest and demonstrates some sense of understanding of the other's viewpoint the more likely it is to be effective. That is to say we employ empathy not just when we are listening but also when we are addressing others or responding to others. This is often described as sensitivity or tact; that we are aware of the impact of our communication on others.

Young children often haven't learned about tact yet and will often embarrass us or get us into trouble with the things they blurt out. However, it is not unusual for adults to come out with insensitive statements that can cause varying degrees of misunderstanding, embarrassment or even hurt.

The key here is to think before you speak (or

write or react through non-verbal cues). To become more adept at responding in this circumstance, practice raising your awareness or consciousness of the inner world of the people you are addressing. There will always be mistakes but most will agree that by taking time to think of others when things get sensitive we will usually communicate more effectively. When we demonstrate pathos when addressing others we are more likely to influence them positively. That is to say when we make an effort to understand and build rapport with the person with whom we are speaking they are more likely to be positively affected by us.

Being clear when we communicate is not always easy. However, the more clearly we communicate our intentions to others the more they will trust us.

Containing the negative

One habit of "letting out" that many of us get into is what I call "stock negative interactive patterns (SNIPs)". These are patterns of negative communication that we and others employ in certain contexts. For example a woman I used to work with made it a habit to complain about the weather every morning. In fact I would argue that this is somewhat of a stock negative interactive pattern in my culture (Ireland) where it can be hard to escape the weather (usually dark and damp) and conversations about it. Another example of a SNIP is to respond to the phrase "how are you?" with an outpouring of how awful you are, or how busy you are, or how stressed you are. I am not saying that one should not talk about these things, it's just that some people make it their habit to always respond in certain conversations like this. The tendency here is that the potential for the conversation to be negative gets a little amplified.

Other stock negative patterns include, bitching about people behind their back, moaning about the job, always making cynical (albeit sometimes funny) remarks (one of my favourites), always playing devil's advocate, always nit-picking or expecting perfection, always taking the underdogs side, complaining about the system, sighing deeply as if you have heard the worst news ever, puffing through the cheeks as if to say, "this is impossible" etc. etc.

It is not to say that any of these behaviours are wrong necessarily, sometimes we need to let off steam. It is just that if they are a default pattern it is likely that your use of them eats at the potential for positive influence. It most likely would be better to find a way to express what is truly bothering you and express the genuine feelings you are feeling. This is difficult because we are less inclined to say things like, "I feel threatened because Susan seems like a very driven manager" or "I am really afraid of what might happen when all these changes come into play" or "I am really angry/sad/hurt that no one acknowledged my birthday"

Often patterns like bitching, gossip and cynicism are just ways of being dishonest about the pain we are experiencing.

Robert Holden captures it nicely in his book

"Happiness Now" when he says,

> By being dishonest about your pain, you stay in pain. Dishonesty may appear to help you get through your day, but it will always leave you in pain at night. Healing is a process of truth, and you cannot get to truth via dishonesty. Dishonesty is, at best, a control tactic, it is not a medicine. It cannot give you peace.

Exercise: Over the next week raise your awareness of some of your stock reactions and responses in different situations. Ask yourself whether or not they are SNIPs. See if you can catch yourself as the week goes on and contain them a little.

"Letting in"

The second part of communication skill is about "letting in". This can be harder than the first part. In fact studies of the brain show that when one is listening the brain has more regions active than when one is talking.

"Letting in" begins with attitude. To really let someone in we need to stop what we are doing and thinking so that you can really listen. We need to be able to show empathy. It sounds easy yet most people on workshops claim they are not good enough at listening and many claim they are rarely genuinely listened to or empathised with.

There is a problem with empathising with someone and that is that we can never be sure if we have got it right. I know more often when I get it wrong than when I get it right. Here are some examples I have experienced that often do not really demonstrate empathy,

"I know just what you mean"

"I know how you feel"

"You poor thing"

"This too will pass"

"There's always someone worse than you"

"I had that very same thing last week"

"At least it's not….."

And one of my favourites after my sister died and I was telling someone about my Mother's pain – "at least she has her other children"

To truly empathise takes effort. Empathy usually involves trying to see the other person's point of view and to get an accurate sense of what they are feeling. When we empathise we try to set aside the way *we* would typically react or interpret events. We then attempt to see how *someone else* would interpret it based on their belief system, their values, their experiences and feelings.

Hearing someone and understanding their perspective and feelings is only part of the process of empathy, however.

The second stage to empathy, and often the piece that is missing, is letting the other person know that we have heard and tried to understand them.

While the first part is difficult because our own ego, personal needs, lack of care, time or resources etc. usually have us paying scant attention to the view point of others, the second stage can be even harder. It is difficult to find the right means to communicate back to someone what we sense they may be going through. However, there is light at the end of the tunnel, the fact is that it is often the effort we put into genuinely trying to empathise that matters more than getting it perfectly right. It is this intimate act of attempting to know what it is like to experience what another is experiencing that contributes to that person feeling empathised with.

This attempt to empathise requires conscious choice. While some of us may have a little more innate abilities in this area we all have to make the conscious decision to set aside our view and try to see that of the other if we want to understand them better. Empathy, then, is a conscious act of choosing to step into the world of the other and letting them know that we are genuinely attempting to see through their eyes.

If someone is in genuine pain, physical, mental or emotional, how can we get it across that we understand their pain and how they are feeling? There is no easy answer here but any attempt is better than a throw away remark or a brushing aside of what is really going on.

Often the process of attempting genuinely to see it through their eyes reveals to us a sense of what to do. In many cases it does not involve words because words can be so limited in communicating the depth of feeling that another person can be experiencing.

Rarely do people tell you in words the depth of a highly emotional experience. They usually let you know through their facial expression or their body language, the tone of their voice or their actions.

Robert Bolton in his excellent book "People Skills" puts it like this,

Non-verbals not only portray a person's feelings, they often indicate how the person is coping with those feelings. For example, the expression on a person's face may indicate that she is angry . The rest of the body shows what she is doing with those angry feelings.

So often our only way of demonstrating that we have heard and tried to understand is through our own body language.

Think back over the last few weeks. How often

has someone really listened to you and understood your point of view? Now, how often has someone felt that you have genuinely listened to and understood them? Would you want them to feel that experience of being understood more from you?

A friend told me once that the intention is more important than the technique. That is to say, if you have an attitude of wanting to listen, empathise and really understand the other this is more important than learning the ten best listening skills all managers or people should use.

So what would that attitude of someone "letting in" and empathizing really be like.

Here is what I have seen people demonstrate in different circumstances while attempting to be empathetic.

- Being relaxed and looking as if they are listening.
- Avoiding or not making assumptions or predicting what the person will say.

- Showing an attitude of openness and non-judgement.
- The eyes appear to be warm and receiving.
- The posture appears to almost mirror that of the other.
- Facial gestures indicate that they are, to some extent, feeling the emotion being expressed – similar to when someone sees a child bang their head badly on a bar or catch their hand in a door – you might see a person who witnesses this showing an ouch on their face.
- Resist the need to be the problem solver unless this is genuinely sought by the other person.
- They seem to resist the need or motivation to interrupt, jump to conclusions or tell their story.
- In some cases they may put into words their sense of what the other person is going through. It might sound like,

"it's as if the world is coming down on top of you right now and you can't get out of its way"

"You seem really frustrated with ...."

"I can't imagine how angry you must feel"

"It seems like it's impossible to cope with it"

Most people who experience lack of empathy and attempts by others to "solve" their problems describe the experience as disempowering.

When trying to listen more empathically it is helpful to show in some way that you have heard. Demonstrate your understanding in some way by either reflecting back your felt sense of what you heard or using appropriate body language or non-verbals. Ask yourself if you can keep the conversation focused on their world a little longer than usual.

If you did not hear correctly or if you tuned out say so and look for clarification. People prefer genuine honesty to pretence.

Give signals to the person that you are paying attention, or show that you want the other person to continue.

Exercise: Think about interactions in which you are required to communicate and ask yourself how much of the following you do.

- Ignoring
- Pretending to listen
- Filtered listening (i.e. listening to the things you want to hear)
- Passive listening (taking in information but not really being there)
- Active or empathic listening.

Over the next week try to make a marked effort to be more empathetic with people in discussions. Say to yourself, "I am going to try to see the world through their eyes and to get a sense of what they are feeling." When you have done this try to communicate your felt sense to the person interacting with you – if you believe it is appropriate to do so.

Keep in mind empathic listening is not always appropriate. However, having some understanding of the other is almost always necessary for good communication to occur.

Credibility review

Score yourself from 1 to 6 (where 6 would be a role model and one is a total beginner) in each area below.

Character,

1. I know my values and work hard at living in accordance with them.
2. I am considered trustworthy by others.
3. I follow through on commitments or promises.
4. I consider the impact of my decisions on others.
5. I am open about my intentions with others.
6. I accept responsibility for myself and my behaviour.
7. I do what is right not just what is popular.

Competence,

1. I complete projects and tasks effectively.
2. I work to expand my knowledge and skill in my area of focus.
3. I focus on the vital and don't get stuck in trivial issues.
4. I manage my time and resources efficiently.
5. I set goals to develop my competence.

6. I deliver high quality work in most circumstances.
7. I am continuously looking for ways to improve my competence and results.

Congruence,

1. People would describe me as very self-aware.
2. I am aware of my feelings, emotions and needs and how they affect my actions.
3. I try to align my inner needs and values with how I express myself.
4. I rarely feel that I am lying to myself or others.
5. Others would describe me as consistent or steady.
6. I find it easy to express when I am conflicted over an issue.
7. My behaviour is an expression of my inner state.

Confidence,

1. I am a good decision maker.
2. I have a strong sense of self belief or self-worth.

3. I can demonstrate humility and do not need to show off my knowledge or expertise.
4. I have little trouble admitting when I am wrong or have made a mistake.
5. While I get anxious about some things it rarely gets in my way or stops me from partaking in things.
6. I am able to confront others in an assertive manner.
7. I find it easy to listen so as to understand others even when I might disagree with their position.

Communication

1. When I listen I fully attend and actively engage with what is being communicated.
2. I am good at empathising or seeing the viewpoint of others.
3. I am good at articulating what I need to say.
4. When communicating to others I am good at assessing whether they are engaged or not from their body language.
5. In most conversations I do about 50% of the talking and 50% of the listening.

6. I would be described by others as a good communicator.
7. When people are talking with me I give them plenty of encouragement and reinforcement through verbal and non-verbal signals.

Tot up your score in each category. Then see if you can use some of the specific statements in this survey to focus on behavioural changes over the next few weeks. Pick only one or two to focus on at a time instead of trying to do all of them. Also look to maximizing those you are good at as well as improving those you are less good at.

Chapter 2

Tip the Ratio

"Every thought is a seed. If you plant crab apples, don't count on harvesting Golden Delicious."

Bill Meyer

"In everyone's life, at some time, our inner fire goes out. It is then burst into flames by an encounter with another human being. We should all be thankful for those people who rekindle the inner spirit."

Albert Schweitzer

I don't think I want to invite John Gottman to dinner. Besides the fact that I don't know him personally and it would be a bit weird, Gottman has become so skilled at studying couples in conversation that from a few minutes observation of their interactions he can, apparently, tell with significant accuracy how long their marriage will last.

Gottman has spent more than 30 years studying couples in action in the Gottman relationship institute. He and his team video couples carrying out various tasks and they then analyse the video frame by frame, categorizing each expressed emotion on the faces of the couples. What they have found is that there is a ratio of 5:1 positive to negative expressed emotions in the better relationships. What's more, these relationships are typically the ones that last.

Marcial Losada and Barbera Frederickson have found a similar ratio in their studies of the performance of teams, in this case the positive to negative ratio is 3:1. Frederickson has also found a similar ratio in her research on students and mental health. That is students who experienced more positive than negative emotions in a ratio of 3:1 tend to show higher scores on social and mental health.

We can have an influence on this ratio by raising our awareness of it and making attempts to tip it in the direction of the positive.

Some people are better at tipping the ratio than others. We have all met the good ones and the bad. The woman or man in the group who seems to be more positive towards us or more encouraging to us, our reaction is usually to respond in kind. Unless of course we are the bitter person who feels put out by the positive inclinations of others.

Perhaps we then fall into the other type of ratio tipper; as someone on one of my workshops once so eloquently put it the "mood hoover". They seem to be able to suck the energy and positivity out of a room. I hope that you are not that person but even if you are, small actions on your part could begin to tip the balance in a more positive direction.

You will probably find that when you think about the ratio you have in relation to people you know, that it varies. With some people you find it easier to be positive than others. The key is to try to build on the ones that have a positive balance and build up the ones that do not. At the very least you can instigate a containment approach, vowing to at least not respond so negatively with the people you find toughest to manage.

Incidental Feedback

On management and leadership development programmes we typically teach people how to give feedback. That is we ask people to observe behaviour and then practice giving specific focused and behaviour based feedback to the person that has been observed. We then ask people to pair up and observe each other throughout a two day period. During this period we ask that they collect specific behaviours that they will give feedback on at the end of the second day. It is a beneficial process and I strongly recommend it to managers in the workplace.

However this is all very well when feedback is consciously thought about and comes from direct observation.

There is another form of feedback that we give

to others almost all of the time. I call this incidental feedback. When negative these are the glances of disapproval, distaste, irritation, frustration and anger that we give off almost instantly when someone is in contravention of our rules. This is the feedback that is harder to change yet it is likely that it is this that creates the real dynamic in business or personal relationships.

Incidental feedback can also be positive. We show empathy for a person who is hurt, we smile as we pass someone by, we show our approval for a person's contribution, we glance fondly at our son or daughter, brother, sister, partner.

John Gottman's studies are based mostly on interpretation of this incidental feedback. My belief is that this positive incidental feedback is giving the other person potentially four things.

1. I see you I acknowledge your presence in the world.
2. I empathise with your situation.

3. I care for you as a person.
4. I approve of you.

Or put in the negative they can potentially communicate,

1. I ignore you or do not acknowledge your presence.
2. I see only my situation.
3. I care little for you.
4. I disapprove of you.

Gottman also refers to the four horsemen of the apocalypse which can contribute to a relationship's decline. These are,

Criticism – Which often means I do not approve of you.

Contempt – I do not care for you as a person.

Defensiveness – I cannot or will not empathise with you because I am too busy defending my ego.

Stonewalling – In defending my ego I will

build a wall of coldness that will make it seem like I do not even see you.

The dangers of ostracism

In a study carried out by Kipling D. Williams and others at Purdue University 1,486 participants were given a computerised ball game to play online with what they believed were other online participants. After a few instances of receiving the ball half of the participants were then deprived of the ball for the rest of the game. After the game all participants were given a test to assess their psychological state. They found that the participants that had been ostracized scored themselves much lower on levels of self-esteem, meaning and their sense of control over their lives. Dr. Williams and his colleagues have carried out numerous similar studies that demonstrate the negative impact of ostracism.

I think there are many times in our lives when we possibly contribute to others feeling ostracized without being consciously aware of it. Increasing our awareness of the feelings and mind-state of others and consciously making an effort not to stonewall others, I believe, can help reduce the likelihood of this happening.

The above is about containing or reducing the negative impact of stonewalling or criticism. We can also broaden and build the positive by purposely going out of our way to encourage the inclusion and participation of others and by tuning into whether or not others might need to be brought into the fold from time to time.

Lack of a good positive to negative ratio along with the abovementioned dynamics are what tend to contribute to a relationship breaking down instead of building up. We can usually see these negative forces as they emerge but it takes conscious, compassionate will-power to make the behavioural shift required to stop them getting their hooks into us and pulling the relationship on a negative course.

We have to choose to contain the inclination to ignore, avenge, cut off, criticize, disapprove of and instead attempt to empathise with the other which can lead to a more compassionate response.

To be on the receiving end of the negative dynamics mentioned above can be fairly crushing for any individual. Given how common they tend to be it is not surprising that people build up the walls that prevent them from finding intimacy and strong lasting relationships

Exercise: Tipping the ratio.

Place your name in a circle at the centre of a page then draw lines connecting a series of circles around that inner circle. Write in the initials of significant people you work with, friends, family, etc. Then consider the last few conversations with each person and write in what your gut tells you the ratio of positive to negative between the two of you may have been. This is not a very objective measure but it will give you a sense of where it lies.

Now ask yourself what you can do to tip the balance of the ones that need to be more positive. Can you consider becoming more aware the next time you are with the person and try to be more positive, encouraging, praising, attentive?

Chapter 3

Project Warmth

"I have learned silence from the talkative, toleration from the intolerant, and kindness from the unkind; yet, strange, I am ungrateful to those teachers."

Kahlil Gibran

"The most precious gift we can offer anyone is our attention"

Thich Nhat Hanh

We all know what it is like to be on the receiving end of someone who barely acknowledges our presence. We tell them something that interests us and their response is a "humph" or a blank expression or if we are really unlucky a look of derision. The sad thing is that we can be so poor at responding with warmth that people will even pay for company who will listen to them.

By telling a story or relating to another in any way we are looking for connection. Many of us seem to have learned that responding with warmth will somehow let us down or be too intimate.

However, when people show warmth to us we tend to engage more fully with them. I have observed that men in business can be quite poor at projecting warmth, yet, it is the more experienced executive, sales person and manager that very often projects a warmth that immediately seems to put you at your ease.

On many training courses with senior managers I have found that it was the leaders who projected warmth and were encouraging of others very often performed more effectively on complex training simulations. In some businesses I have worked with I have sometimes wondered did I miss a sign at the front door that said all smiling during the hours of 8.30 and 5.00 will elicit disciplinary action or any acts of encouragement or praise will be frowned upon until fully eliminated. It is as if to pretend we are human with very human needs in this place where we spend a large proportion of our life is unlawful.

Not all businesses are the same. Like the way restaurants and hotels can get the customer service atmosphere right, so too can some businesses with their staff. These businesses that demonstrate a warmth and atmosphere of encouragement appear to value themselves, their staff and their customer and it is demonstrated in their behaviour to one another and even at times to myself as a consultant.

The 4 Ms

The four Ms is a simple but effective way of thinking about how we approach situations and how we leave our mark on others. In almost all interactions we leave a symbolic or mental mark on the person or people with whom we have interacted. The question is: what mark do you leave? The mark we leave is a result of the method of interaction that we have chosen. This method or set of behaviours has arisen out of a mind-set or set of thoughts, beliefs and values and that mind-set is very often influenced by our mood or our underlying feeling or attitudinal state.

So it might look like the diagram below.

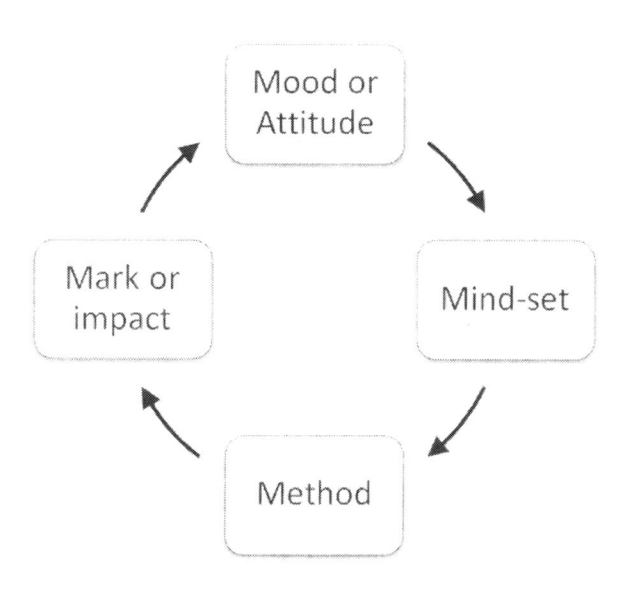

Mood or Attitude → Mind-set → Method → Mark or impact → Mood or Attitude

In looking at the above model you will probably notice that there are two Ms over which we have more control: these are the mind-set and the method. We can never tell exactly what result (mark) will ensue from our behaviour, and our moods and feelings can be strongly influenced by a variety of things only one of which is our thinking. However, keep in mind that our thinking can influence our mood so we do at least have some influence here.

Inherent within this model is the idea that our mind-set or mental frame of ourselves and the world is likely to influence how we interact with the world (psychologists call this "cognitive bias"). Over the last fifty years or so neuroscientists and psychologists have repeatedly demonstrated that there is a correlation between the way we view and interpret the world and how well we manage stress, change or crisis.

For example, Psychologist Michael Eyesenck has shown that when people hear isolated words that have the same sound but different meaning (for example dye and die, steal and steel, pain and pane) and are asked to write the words down, people who score high on anxiety scales are more likely to write down the spelling with the negative connotation.

In another study recently reported in Scientific American Mind participants in the study were given a so called performance improvement hormone. This was a double blind study, so half of the participants were given a placebo (a pill with no active ingredient). The researchers asked all participants to guess whether they were on the real drug or not. In cases where participants on the placebo (i.e. did not receive the drug) guessed they were on the real drug there was a significant improvement on four fitness tests measuring strength, endurance, power and ability to sprint. It seems their belief alone was what had contributed to this improvement.

These kinds of studies continue to be carried out in various ingenious ways and time and again they show the strength of the impact of mental interpretation on human behaviour.

Possibly one of the most famous of these studies on mind-set and its relation to influence was carried out by Robert Rosenthall and Lenore Jacobson in 1968. They showed that young children's performance could be significantly affected by the expectations held by their teachers. When teachers were told that children who scored higher on a specific test (later shown to be indicative of nothing at all) were likely to show great improvement over time those children did in fact show significant progress, in some cases moving to the top of their class.

Mental models

Our mind-set is like a mental model or cognitive carving that we have made of ourselves, others and the world around us. They are a representation of the thing and not the actual thing itself. The accuracy or the reality of the representation is not always very solid and in many cases can be quite warped.

Given the mind's tendency to absorb information and form quite warped viewpoints I think it is essential to try and become aware, first of all, of the mind-sets and mental models we are using to interpret who we are, secondly the mental models we are using to see others and thirdly the mental models we are using to attempt to have an influence on others and the world around us.

Our mental models of who we are and how we typically behave can be strongly rooted in the past. These mental models have often been based on information and feedback received at vulnerable times in our childhood and adolescence. It is somewhat like an old black and white movie portraying us as the stereotypical bad boy/girl, idiot, saviour, grumpy child etc.

If our mental models are outdated or inaccurate then we need to remould them. Perhaps even begin to shift that cognitive bias a little towards the positive. Don't get me wrong I do not think we should all ignore reality and become delusional but I do think that our negative cynical mind-sets can often be just as delusional as ones that are tipped in the positive. In fact research would appear to hold that a somewhat overly positive mind-set is healthier than a somewhat negative one.

The power of refinement

Our minds are wonderful things. We are able to take a simple object and generalize it up to a more complex one. Read the two words below quickly and without thinking about it.

THE CAT

In the words our mind tends to at first see the words THE CAT. It is usually only our second response to notice that the H and the A are actually the same symbol. This is one of the brilliant feats of intelligence that we are capable of.

Without this ability to generalise things we would find it very hard to survive in the modern world. We are constantly putting things into their context so as to make sense of them. However, in some cases this contextualizing and generalising does not always pay off. We often generalise about ourselves, for example, saying things like, *"I don't understand politics or music or mathematics etc"*. When in fact what is usually the case is that we either don't like these facets of life or we have taken very little time to either study them or get to know them. However, we have somehow convinced our logical brain that instead of these being assumptions or generalisations they are actually facts. Thus our behaviour can be guided with some conviction.

We do a similar thing with others often in the negative. "I don't like her she's mean" or "I hate solicitors" or "I think men are dreadful drivers".

Generalising too much about ourselves or others usually leads to prejudice which can often lead to negative influence.

If we could catch ourselves when we use generalisations and attempt to refine our current mind-set or definition of the way things are I believe we move one step closer to a more enlightened mind. Chunking down questions can help take us from a general frame to a more specific one. For example you find yourself saying, "I hate the way you always interrupt me in the middle of sentences" you could ask yourself, "is it really always or just sometimes? When does he interrupt? Is it when he can't seem to get a word in edgeways? Is it just the odd time? If I was to give more specific feedback on this issue what would it be?

Exercise: Try to catch yourself over the next few days generalizing about yourself or others. Ask yourself, "how can I get more specific about this, how can I refine my frame or definition?"

Exercise: If you were to be characterized in a movie what qualities would stand out? Would this be an accurate portrayal of you?

What negative beliefs or frames of yourself do you think you need to let go of?

What might a more realistic picture look like?

What would a more positive or stronger picture of you look like?

Exercise: Think about someone with whom you have a negative relationship. How would you describe your view of this person?

Is it possible that the frame you put around this person tends to contribute to the negativity of the relationship?

Is there any way that you could adjust your frame and tilt it towards the positive? For example could you think of any of their good points or strengths?

Can you think of anything you like about them?

Can you think about their intention and whether it might be positive for them even though it may not seem positive to you? Are they really all bad or does thinking about them that way just make it easier for you to not build a relationship with them?

Leaving your mark

In terms of the interactional mental or emotional marks we leave with others we could divide them into three broad categories,

Marks that are neutral.

Marks that leave damage.

Marks that encourage or empower the other.

Exercise: Leaving your mark

Consider the last time you left a mark that caused a little damage.

What was the impact?

What method, behaviour or action did you utilise?

What was your mind-set, what were you thinking or believing at that time?

What was your mood, feeling or underlying need?

In order to leave a mark that would be more encouraging or empowering for the other, what could you change – mood, mind-set, method? And how would you change it?

Now think of someone with whom you want to leave a more positive mark.

What effect do you want to have on them?

What method will help you to have this effect?

What mind-set/thinking/beliefs/values will guide your methods?

What mood would best suit your mind-set? What feelings can you draw on?

For the above feelings/mood consider drawing on your memory of a situation where you had the feeling. Usually when we remember a feeling we actually experience it, in part, in the present moment.

Projecting Warmth

In projecting warmth I do not mean a false projection of feelings that aren't there, similar to what some politicians might do. I mean trying to find a connection to the need for belonging within you and becoming aware of that need in others. The best way of thinking of it is to notice the genuine warmth that a new mother will often show to their baby or to notice the way people respond when a small baby smiles or when we see someone we love that we haven't seen for a long time. This is a natural response to the human need for connection. Many of us have buried this far down in our psyche under layers of unhappiness, resentment and cynicism. It takes a conscious willful effort to bring it back up to the surface, with some it might take a long time but most of us do remember how eventually.

Exercise: Consider your day to day interactions with, customers, colleagues, bosses, subordinates, family and friends. How warm do you think you come across on a scale of 1 to

10 where 10 is very warm?

In what specific situations do you need to project a little more warmth?

How might you do this?

Do you fear projecting warmth?

What are you afraid might happen?

Projecting warmth can take practice if it doesn't come naturally to you, at first it may feel false but if your intention is genuine the results are usually worth it.

Conscious Feedback

Believe it or not we humans thrive on feedback. We get it constantly from our environment; turn a key and the lock opens, press the button and the TV comes on. Every day we perform actions and we get natural feedback that lets us know whether our behaviour is getting us what we want or not.

Feedback reinforces behaviour and generally should let us know when we need to change our behaviour so as to get a different result. If we flip the switch on the wall and the light goes on we move on to our next action. If, however, we flip the switch and the room remains dark we then need to adapt and seek an alternative way to light the room or change the bulb.

Verbal and non-verbal feedback are two of our most fundamental tools for effective communication. Let's start with non-verbal feedback.

Non-verbal feedback:

Non-verbal feedback is all of those subtle cues that people give us to encourage us to continue talking or to stop talking or to be careful about what we say or even to not dare say what we said again.

It is the look and expression we give, the body language we use and adapt as a conversation progresses. From an objective position it looks like nods, facial gestures, posture, the turn of the body, the tilt of the head, the twitch of the nose and many other subtle things that we do not notice. If non-verbal feedback is in tune with the other there is usually rapport or a sense of resonance. When non-verbal feedback is out of tune there is usually a break in rapport or dissonance. A good example of this would be when we are talking to someone about a topic that we feel strongly about. If the person agrees or is empathising effectively we will usually perceive this in their eyes and their demeanour. If, however, they suddenly disagree with something we say we often notice an immediate change in their eyes. One minute they are with us the next minute they have cut off, usually their mind-set has shifted and so their listening behaviour shifts as well, most likely they are preparing their rebuttal or perhaps deciding whether or not to verbally disagree with what has been said.

If we could adopt an approach "letting in" while someone is talking, a belief that it is not essential, while this person is talking, to either agree nor disagree just to listen and understand we might have a better chance of keeping rapport. If we keep rapport we have a better chance of influencing the other. Note I said neither agree nor disagree, simply work to understand. I am very aware that this is easier said than done. However, I am also aware that when I adopt this approach myself it usually works and I have also observed it often in others.

There is one caveat and it involves something I mentioned earlier: it is important that our intention be to genuinely understand the other person. The intention is more important than the technique. The intention is at the root of the credibility pyramid whereas the communication technique is at the tip. In the short term people may be fooled by a clever technique but most people will pick up on our true intentions.

I experienced a good example of this a number of years ago. I was in my kitchen having a heated discussion with my wife. After a little while she turned to me and said, "I am not talking to you about this anymore". I was shocked, disappointed and a little angered. I genuinely believed I was really listening and trying to understand her point of view. I said, "why won't you talk to me about it?" She said, "because you've gone into counsellor mode". I tried to quell my anger for a moment – I mean I was doing all the right things here. I was listening, nodding, rephrasing, showing that I was hearing what she was saying and making sure I really understood by summarising what I was hearing. There was one problem: I was doing all of this so as to win the argument. When I examined my intentions I realised I was using all of these techniques I had learned to sway the argument in my direction. Internally I guess I was saying, "make her feel like you have heard and understood then demonstrate through your linguistic brilliance (ha, ha) how irrational her thinking is". Well I guess I was caught. I was using a car salesman technique to try to get my wife to buy into my way of thinking.

So you can see why the congruence level is so difficult. Flawed attempts at genuine understanding will nearly always succeed over silky smooth attempts at winning people over, at least if we want to have lasting relationships of trust.

You probably know of people to whom you find it easy to talk. You probably also know people who will give you nothing but a blank stare yet will say they are listening. Let's hope you are not one of those people. However, if you are it is not too late to change. You can always become more aware of the signals you give off when people talk to you. If you are the person who sits with a blank expression you can learn to nod occasionally or give an "mm –hmm".

Exercise : Ask yourself what it is like to be on the receiving end of you in a conversation. Think of a colleague with whom you work. How rewarding is it for them to talk with you in typical conversations? How much do you give them purely in terms of nonverbal cues? Are there specific ways that you can choose to be more encouraging?

Verbal feedback.

When considering giving verbal feedback we should first of all ask ourselves what we hope to achieve by giving feedback on this particular occasion.

C.U.B.E.S. is an acronym that I use to make criticism constructive.

In other words is your feedback going to be credible, useful, behavioural, evidence-based, specific. You should also ask yourself whether the time is right and whether the environment or context is also right. For more on the cubes acronym see chapter 6.

As a rule we should try to get into the habit of giving a lot more positive feedback than negative feedback. There is some research that shows a 4 to 1 ratio is best.

Here is a method or process which can be useful when thinking about giving feedback.

1. Make your feedback based on observed behaviour. For example, "I see you've finished the project on time", or to be more specific, "I see you've finished the training project on time".
2. Offering your interpretation or thoughts on what you've observed. For example, "I see you finished the new training project on time I think you showed real initiative and were very pro-active."
3. Say how you feel about what you've observed. For example, "I was really pleased" or "I am delighted".
4. State your expectations for the future. For example, "I hope it goes as well for you next time".

The feedback doesn't have to be exactly in the above order just as long as you are specific and base it on what you have actually observed rather than making it generalised and nonspecific. A very common habit is for people to just say well done or that's great. When we take the time to give genuine positive feedback that is specific and based on what we have seen and experienced, people are more likely to feel prized and encouraged.

A similar process can be used for negative feedback, again making it as specific as possible and focusing on behaviour not on the person. Remember most people want to build healthy honest personal and working relationships, it is virtually impossible to do this without occasionally giving some negative feedback. It is also essential for our personal credibility to be able to give negative feedback. People are less likely to respect us if we keep hiding the truth about how we feel.

Here is an example of the same process used to give negative feedback,

"I noticed six spelling errors on the presentation you prepared for the management meeting later on today. I think it's important for the presentation's credibility that it be free from errors. If you could take a look at it and correct those errors that would be great."

In some cases when giving feedback it may not be essential or appropriate to describe how we feel. We may find it better to just focus on what we observed and our interpretation of the situation. For example, "That's the third time you have interrupted me in the last few minutes, I find it rude and disrespectful. Could you please wait until I have finished to interject."

However where work is concerned a good general rule of thumb is to try to get into the habit of expressing how you feel when you're describing good performance or people performing at their best.

The order of the feedback can be jumbled around quite a bit.

Here's another example,

"I love the way you used graphics on the current issue of the company magazine. I think it really brought some of the articles to life. It would be great if all of the issues could look as professional and engaging as that."

Chapter 4

Empower Others

"It is not power that corrupts but fear. Fear of losing power corrupts those who wield it and fear of the scourge of power corrupts those who are subject to it."

Aung San Suu Kyi

"Nearly all men can stand adversity, but if you want to test a man's character, give him power."

Abraham Lincoln

In any interaction you can be either building up or breaking down it is rare that conversations are completely neutral.

There are many different types of power in human relations, some of them are synopsized below

Position power – This kind of power is based on our rank or position in a system or organisation.

When it is disempowering: When we use it to enlist people into doing what they should not, cannot do or would prefer not to do. An extreme example would be a soldier being forced to commit an act that they find reprehensible.

When it can be empowering: When we need to enforce discipline particularly in start-up situations when ground rules are not the norm. I would use my position as trainer to bring a group to order in a workshop or to guide the group in establishing ground rules.

Coercive power – that which we take based on our superior wealth, strength and in some cases position.

When it is disempowering: As we are being coerced it is nearly always disempowering to a lesser or greater degree.

Stephen Covey describes coercive power in his book Principle Centred Leadership,

"The leader in this case has created a fear in the follower that either something bad is going to happen to them or something good will be taken away from them if they do not comply………….But their commitment is superficial and their energies can quickly turn to sabotage and destruction 'when no one is looking'." - Principle Centred Leadership, Stephen Covey

We tend to use coercive power either when we know no better or we believe we must have complete control or compliance. Many will argue against this kind of power but unfortunately many also resort to it particularly in difficult or crisis type situations.

The impact of continuous coercive power is a culture of dependence where there will be little if any autonomy and creativity, initiative and differential effort (where one pushes the boat out to achieve something) are rarely ever seen.

However, in some contexts it is seen as more acceptable, the military for example or when it is genuinely for the sake of a person's health or well-being.

When it can be empowering: It may make sense if we have enlisted someone to use this approach. For example, a fitness coach we have purposely employed to help enforce a fitness regime or if we wish to be disempowered, paradoxically, some people can find this idea stimulating.

Utility power – Power conferred on us because we have something someone else wants.

When it is disempowering: When the person

uses that something against us. For example, blackmail or when the person refuses to carry out a transaction just so that they can revel in the power they hold over us. Or when the person chooses to monopolize a market place because they have the utility and there is a very strong demand for it.

When it can be empowering: When simple negotiations and transactions need to take place and they do in an ethical and fair way. For example the electric company has the power to provide us with electricity as long as we are willing to pay for it.

Relational power – Power we have because of who we know.

When it is disempowering: When we use our connections to others as a way of standing apart. We do this in many different ways whether it's the club we belong to or the "important" people we know. When we use our relationships to discriminate we are usually saying, "look I am connected and you are not". This form of power can be particularly damaging at its extreme because it can lead to a level of elitist tribalism. We are not part of the group so we matter less or we are a figure of discrimination, ridicule or even violence.

When it can be empowering: It can be empowering when used as a tool of inclusion rather than exclusion; when it fosters collaboration in teams, groups, tribes; when it brings people together to share a meaningful dialogue or action. Relational power is social conformity at its best, binding people who gather for a common purpose. Nelson Mandela when speaking about his achievements often talks about the power of the collective, making it clear that it is only through relationship that his goals and the goals of his party would have been achieved.

Knowledge or expert power – Power based on us having knowledge or capability in an area that others do not.

When it is disempowering: When we use our knowledge or expertise to get the better of others or to show others up. When we act as if having knowledge, expertise, insight proves us better than others. When we hoard knowledge as if to say, "I know this and you don't therefore I am better than you". This kind of power is often abused in business situations and probably contributes significantly to reduced trust and low psychological safety. If we do not communicate what we know to others then people begin to get suspicious.

When it can be empowering: When used to benefit others or when used to teach others in a way that they find useful. As long as we believe that having knowledge or expertise makes us better than anyone in some way we are taking an unequal stance. If we can let go of the need to be better than others and see our knowledge and/or expertise as a way to serve others, to guide others or to help where help is needed then we can use knowledge based power more effectively.

Reward power – based on rewards that we can provide that may be wanted by another. Attention and approval are also in themselves a reward in some circumstances.

When it is disempowering: When we know we can give a reward or a reinforcement but we either don't bother or don't want to let people have it. It can be as simple as an acknowledgement with a smile or a nod of the head sometimes.

When it can be empowering: When given

appropriately for a job well done or a service provided or in the case of children, behaviour that we deem appropriate.

Charismatic power – based on the interpersonal power or personal magnetism that we may have when communicating with others.

When it is disempowering: It is difficult to explain what charismatic power is exactly but I have little doubt that some have a lot of it and some have little or none. It can be disempowering when used to lure people in and subsequently use them to suit our needs. Some people are charmed more easily than others and people with a high level of charisma often see this and sometimes use it to their advantage. Charismatic power is disempowering purely because at its root it is about having a power over people. If you have a power over me then it goes without saying that I have given up some of my power over myself.

When it can be empowering: I am not sure it can ever be empowering for those who fall under its spell because of its very nature. However, that is not to say that it cannot serve people in a benevolent way. There may be times where a leader or influencer needs to draw in a crowd so as to unite them in a common purpose. There may be times when a teacher needs to use their personal magnetism to engage a classroom. Dare I say it there may even be times when a little personal magnetism can serve us in finding a partner. The difficulty lies in the follow through and whether it is all we have.

Decisional power – based on who has the power in a given circumstance to make the decisions.

When it is disempowering: When we keep it in almost all circumstances. In other words we never let others have the power to decide. We were given or earned this power and so we want to keep it; it's what proves our worth or what shows us to be better than all the rest.

When it can be empowering: When we use it effectively to make good decisions that are of benefit to all. Also when we give it away appropriately. It may be appropriate to let a small child decide what they would like for lunch but it may not be appropriate if they keep choosing sweets. Similarly in work situations people may need the knowledge and expertise before they can make effective and informed decisions.

Conferred or Permission power – Power freely given to us by others.

When it is disempowering: When it is given by one person and not by another yet we need to influence both. For example if you manage a team and some members will not grant you permission to lead them. In this case you usually have to take the time to build your credibility with this person or at worst use your position power with them.

When it is empowering – When it is freely given and people have genuinely designated you as the one to lead. Where goals are shared.

Each one of these can have an empowering or disempowering effect on the people we influence.

I think the key to improving our use of power so as to become a more positive influencer is down to when we hold on to power and when we let it go.

Ask yourself the following,

In each of the above forms of power when do I keep it and when do I let it go?

In each case ask yourself whether you could let go a little more or whether there are some situations where you are letting go a little too much.

In some cases empowering others may mean taking control of a situation. For example if you know that someone is having a heart attack and there is no time to explain to others you will likely choose a mixture of position power and coercive power to influence people to follow you or do what you say. However, if you are delegating a task that someone has to do and they know how to do it then you want them to have the decision power to complete the task.

Exercise: To understand a little more about disempowering others try the following exercise.

Write down as many things as you can think of that you find disempowering yourself, now think of any other ways you might be aware of and possibly any that you have experienced, say from your boss or your doctor or even your parents.

Here are some examples that I have come across,

- Finishing a job for someone who you know is quite capable.
- Doing too much.
- Not letting go of the responsibility for doing a task.
- Interrupting.
- Not giving your attention.
- Not listening when you know you should.
- Keeping someone dependent on you by doing almost everything for them.
- Talking with an air of authority on any subject.
- Always being the one who takes control.
- Giving away power but doing it in a condescending way.
- Treating people like children.

Become aware of the power sources within you; the power to choose your response, the power to let go and the power to give away power.

Empowered delegation

When delegating a task or teaching a new skill think about how you can make it empowering for the other person.

I find it usually helpful to go through the 4Ws and H in relation to the task. This stands for,

Why: Why is it important for this task to be done by this person?

What: What is the specific result or outcome you are looking for? What standards have to be met?

When: By when does the outcome need to be achieved?

Who: Who will do what, specifically. Who will be responsible and who will be accountable for the work to be completed?

How: How should the task be down? Are there previous efficient and effective methods for achieving the task (in Intel the call this BKMs or Best Known Methods)? How much flexibility does the person have in doing the task? How much control can you give the person?

The stages of learning and delegation

It is also useful to consider the stage of learning and development at which the person being delegated to is.

People typically go through a number of stages of development from absolute beginner to expert when learning a new task or skill. If we can modify our approach to teaching, managing or coaching as the person goes through these stages then the experience for them is less likely to be disempowering and more likely to give them a sense that they are getting what they need at each stage.

Stage 1. Unconscious incompetence is when a person has never done a task before and therefore does not yet know how difficult it might be. Learning to drive is a good example. Most people are not aware of the true difficulty of this task until they begin to try it themselves, similarly learning a musical instrument, a new computer programme or a craft are like this. It is usually only when we begin to try a complex skill that we realise how ignorant or inept we truly are.

At stage one a person usually needs to be given clear instruction on what needs to be done and how it should be done to achieve the best result. Clear, direct yet patient teaching and guidance are what is required for the person to feel empowered. The person who does not get clear guidance is like the person who opens a flat pack piece of furniture and finds all the bits but no instructions (or instructions in a foreign language).

When we begin to gain this realisation of our own incompetence we have entered the stage of conscious incompetence; we now realise the complexity of the task and the mountain that has to be climbed in order to gain competence. This usually has a dampening effect on our enthusiasm and over time without assistance can lead to significant frustration and often resignation or just quitting.

Stage 2. Conscious incompetence. At this stage we usually feel our highest level of anxiety and frustration. The task can appear impossible or overwhelming, remember learning to drive or trying to understand algebra? We can feel like we may never get beyond the beginner stage and our inner motivation can be telling us that the end result is not worth the effort. This is often the stage where young children (and many adults) give up trying to learn a musical instrument or how to dance or knit or paint.

This giving up is a pity, because if the right approach had been taken, the right guidance given, they might have stayed the course. Unfortunately too often people describe how their teacher just got stricter and more impatient when they reached this stage. In fact the teacher himself is just displaying his own frustration and indicating their stage of development in relation to the skill of teaching.

What is needed is patient re-teaching and an encouraging voice that shows belief in the learner's ability to stick with it and learn what has to be learned. The effective teacher, coach, manager or even parent will reinforce (praise) each successful move and gently redirect or reteach each incorrect one.

I saw this with my son's violin teacher, how he showed patience and a firm resolution so that my son would break through each learning barrier as he learned his instrument (unlike his father I should add). This is no mean task when it comes to the violin as anyone who has experienced the sound of tortured cats/nails on a blackboard that emanates from the young learners violin will tell you.

Stage 3. Conscious competence. As a learner begins to follow the correct steps and judiciously gets the task done correctly they show progress. In the early stages, however, this is usually achieved in a conscious, attentive manner. Full attention is still required.

The new driver still has to think about each gear change, the new musician has to focus on each note, the computer programmer checks and rechecks that they wrote the code correctly. This is where the teacher or guide or manager begins slowly to pull away, encouraging the consciously competent learner to go it alone a little at a time.

They have broken the back of learning the steps now they just have to practice it again and again and again. In some cases this comes fairly quickly: maybe learning to cook a simple meal, for example. In other cases it might take 10,000 hours: learning to become an accomplished orchestral musician, or a skilled pilot. The danger here is that a person becomes dependent on the guide or teacher and doesn't make the jump to going it alone. Often parents can find it hard at this stage to let their children go it alone. However, this dependence will tend to lead to disempowerment.

It is worth noting that empowerment is not the same as a state of contentment or zero anxiety. Sometimes empowerment can have an anxiety associated with it because it means we are the responsible ones, we are holding the reins and we are outside of our comfort zone, competent but not fully confident. However, good guidance and coaching can serve to ease that anxiety.

Stage 4. Unconscious competence. When a person has begun to be able to perform a task without having to think about it they are now committing it to procedural, habitual memory. The task is second nature to them and while not easy their skill level now matches the complexity of the task. They now need to be able to really go it alone, starting new similar tasks, adapting the way the task is done, innovating new ways of achieving task results.

At this stage they need to be given autonomy and be allowed to manage themselves, with the teacher or guide only stepping in occasionally to offer a little encouragement and to hone and refine the skills involved.

When using the above it is important to discuss (except maybe in the case of children) each stage with the learner and agree how guidance is given throughout. The more the person feels they are involved in their own development the more empowered they are likely to feel. Many acts of disempowerment could be avoided if just a little more involvement in the process was provided by the person with the knowledge or position power. The manager, teacher or guide should look for regular feedback on their approach and well it is working for the learner, employee or student.

The managers who have the humility and the courage to ask their staff the question, "how am I doing?" and who genuinely listen and accept the answers they get, in my experience are often the ones who stand out. That willingness to see their staff as their best customers seems to have significant effect on their perceived credibility and their positive to negative ratio.

Exercise: Whether you are a manager, a teacher or a parent when delegating a task or teaching a new skill ask yourself the following,

1. What stage of learning is this person at in relation to this skill?
2. How do I need to teach or coach this person to empower them at this stage and to facilitate their development to the next stage?

Chapter 5

Establish Clear Boundaries

(But not brick walls)

"To know oneself, one should assert oneself."

Albert Camus

"If you want to make peace with your enemy, you have to work with your enemy. Then he becomes your partner."

Nelson Mandella

Clear boundaries are set when we are assertive with others, taking a genuine stance of I'm OK and Your OK. It is not about being aggressive or selfish but about having a clear and confident respect for yourself and for others. Most of the time we are unaware of when our psychological boundaries are fuzzy or unclear.

Our default repertoire of general behaviour is laid down over years and so much of our interactions are habitual and unconscious that it can be difficult knowing when we are and when we are not setting clear boundaries with others. If we are lucky our genes, personality and life learning have granted us a natural ability to set boundaries but in many cases this is not the case. When times get tough or emotions run high or we are staring in the face of manipulative or aggressive behaviour our lack of clear boundaries becomes more evident.

Here are some examples of fuzzy boundaries.

- Being unable to say no without an excuse.
- Feeling we are responsible for the mood or feelings of others.
- Feeling we need to constantly gain the approval of others.
- Almost always feeling we have to explain or excuse our behaviour.
- Acting so as to rescue others in situations where they need to rescue themselves.

- Feeling we cannot hear others express difficult emotions because of how it will make us feel.
- Cutting off from others when emotions run high or we feel hurt.
- Not allowing others know how we feel for fear we will appear vulnerable.
- Unable to state our preferences.
- Not being aware of the negative impact our expression of feelings may be having on others.
- Constantly letting others know how we feel.
- Manipulating others to get what we want.
- Regularly turning up late or letting others down and blaming it on other events.
- Constantly turning up early for fear we might be late and lose the approval of others.
- Wanting others to take care of us when we really need to take care of ourselves.
- Constantly doing things for others to show our generosity but underneath resenting that we don't receive in return.

- Always needing to be in control and dismissing situations or people where we cannot be in control.
- Unable to commit and stay the course with anything.

Here are some examples of healthy boundaries

- Being able to say no because we need to or want to.
- Feeling responsible and acting responsibly with regard to our mood or feelings.
- Noticing the desire for approval but not letting it influence how we act.
- Explaining and excusing when it is needed or asked for.
- Being compassionate and caring with others while accepting they are responsible for themselves.
- Acknowledging that it is difficult to hear others distress while attempting to empathise where possible.
- Staying the course with others when emotions run high or we feel hurt.
- Choosing when it is appropriate to let others know how we feel even when we fear appearing vulnerable.

- Realising that it is more helpful to others when we state our preferences and acting accordingly.
- Raising our awareness of the negative impact our expression of feelings may be having on others and containing this when necessary.
- Attuning ourselves to the state of others and choosing when it is appropriate to let others know how we feel.
- Asking openly for what we want and letting go or striving harder when we don't get it.
- When turning up late we acknowledge it and accept responsibility ourselves.
- Raising our awareness of our need to be early and not letting it govern our behaviour.
- Taking care of ourselves, asking for care when we genuinely need it and not expecting others to read our minds or instinctively know when we are in need.
- Doing things for others out of genuine compassion and letting go of conditions or expectations.
- Raising our awareness of our need for control and accepting that in most cases we cannot be fully in control. Avoiding

letting our need for control dictate how we interact with the world. Accepting change as a natural part of life.
- Becoming aware of our fear of commitment. Learning to let go and stay the course.

Healthy boundaries are about approaching the world with all that we have got, letting go of old voices that tell us we are not good enough or we should be ashamed and accepting that we are adult human beings who are grappling with what it is to be human. Instead of accepting our basic humanity much of the time we spend our lives in a state of feeling or believing that we are more than human or less than human.

Here are some examples of what I mean,

Less than human:
I am not good enough.
I will be found out.
I am afraid to tell you who I am.
I shouldn't show my feelings.
No one would really pick me.

More than human:
I am better than others.
I must appear strong at all times.
I never make mistakes and if I do I pretend I do not.
I appear in control always.
When wearing my serious hat I must never appear foolish.
I must at all times either be fully knowledgeable or be dismissively ignorant.

Human:
I am good enough.
I can show my vulnerabilities.
I can make mistakes.
I do not have to hide my flaws, weaknesses or strengths.
I can assert myself without feeling guilty, defensive or angry.
It is normal to sometimes feel out of control.
I can let myself and others down and still be OK.
I can change my mind.
I can say I am sorry.

Healthy boundaries are about acceptance of who we are, perfect and imperfect at the same time. Realising that for this short term on earth we have been given a set of genes and a context in which to operate at our best if we choose to do so.

It also means we accept responsibility for ourselves and we work at understanding and respecting the boundaries of others conscious that they will not always meet our expectations and we will not always meet theirs.

Essentially healthy boundaries tend to culminate in assertiveness. Below I have outlined what it means to be both assertive and non-assertive.

Being assertive:

When we are assertive we typically balance our own needs with that of the other person. We are happy to state our opinion, viewpoint, needs, feelings and values and we will choose to do so in a way that is considerate of others.

When we are assertive we also take responsibility for ourselves in all respects and do not expect others to take care of us unless they have contracted to do so. This is difficult because it means not being able to say, "you made me feel ………". To suggest that someone else makes us feel something is to suggest that they can get into our body and alter our body chemistry. A more assertive option is to state, "When you …….. I feel………" So for example, "when you shout at me I feel threatened."

When being assertive, people will also refrain from trying to control the behaviours of others or dominate others in relationships.

Responsibility in this context means accepting that while we are influenced by others and our context we ourselves are ultimately responsible for our behaviours, feelings and thoughts. When influencing and negotiating, assertiveness will help us to approach with a mind-set of I'm OK and you're OK and/or find a mutual solution whereby we both can benefit.

An assertive person is not an aggressive person. An assertive person sees the importance of their own needs but also sees how their needs in most cases are met alongside the needs of others. When people are assertive they will generally go for a collaborative form of influence or negotiation but they may if necessary become commanding or directive if this seems like the most beneficial course, all things being equal. For example if we know there is a fire in the building and we need to clear people out as quickly as possible we are more likely to take on a commanding approach. The main thing to remember is that this is a choice we are making not a default style of influence.

Being aggressive:

When we are aggressive we are generally stuck in our own point of view, thinking the world revolves around us or at least can be made to. We rarely think of the other person's needs, opinions, feelings or values.

Aggression usually involves an effort to control others and get them to act so as to live up to our expectations or fulfil our needs.

When aggressive we often use our emotional, physical, positional or intellectual power to overwhelm the other so that they will give in to our way of thinking or behaving. When influencing with aggression our mind-set is usually I'm OK and you're NOT OK and negotiations are competitive and driven by a win – lose approach.

There are many ways to be aggressive other than loud voice or strong words. People can become very aggressive through the clever use of intellect. We sometimes see this with media journalists and politicians.

Being passive:

When we are passive we tend to fall in with the status quo and flow with the direction of the prevailing wind. Our concern is generally keeping the peace and not upsetting anyone, especially ourselves. We are happy to let others lead and will often subordinate our own opinions, values, needs and even feelings to others.

When being passive we are usually convincing ourselves that we are being caring but rarely admitting that it is our fear of standing up for ourselves and our fear of confrontation that is really driving us. In situations involving influence and negotiation we often give in or acquiesce to the needs of others tending to think I'm not OK you are OK and ending up with a lose- win outcome.

Passive is not the same as peaceful or non-violent it is closer to submissive in this context and usually means the needs of the passive person are given second place to the needs of the other.

Being passive-aggressive

When we are passive-aggressive we usually have a strong desire to have things done our way but we do not have the courage or compassion to use overt force or direct methods, instead we opt for more subtle and duplicitous methods.

Sarcasm, cynicism, victimisation and emotional blackmail are some of the common tools of passive-aggression. We take indirect pot shots at colleagues, friends, family or we play manipulative games in order to get our point across and our needs met.

If verbal violence and attack are the tools of aggression, silence, stonewalling, gossip and snide remarks are common tools of passive-aggression. The mind-set of passive-aggression is often I'm OK - you're not OK or sometimes I'm not OK – you're not OK and the outcome is usually lose-lose.

Exercise: Questions to consider in regard to assertiveness,

If aggression is an issue

In what situations do you tend to use aggressive behaviour? What typically triggers this? Who typically is hurt by your aggression? What new thinking or behaviour can you put in place so as not to choose an aggressive response? If you were to physically train yourself what would you physically need to do (for example, take a deep breath, count to 10, relax, leave the room etc.)?

If being passive is an issue

In what situations are you likely to use passive behaviour? What typically triggers this? What new thinking or behaviour can you put in place so as not to choose a passive response? What would this look like if you perfected it?

If being passive-aggressive is an issue

In what situations are you likely to use passive-aggressive behaviour? What typically triggers this? Who typically gets hurt when you choose this kind of response? Are there any new behaviours you could use the next time you feel inclined to go for passive-aggression?

In what specific situations do you need to be more assertive? What do you need to tell yourself in order to be more assertive?

Assertive stance:
- Confident mind-state & self talk
- Courage & Compassion
- Willingness to ask for what we need
- Willingness to let go when necessary

Confident mind-state & self-talk: Our mind-state and what we say to ourselves influences us in every moment of every day. Every action we take and every word we say is preceded by a mental state of one kind or another. The challenge is that much of this is subconscious and out of our present moment awareness. Research has shown that our subconscious can be influenced in a variety of different ways. For example, in one study subjects were shown pictures of faces with strong emotional expressions. The length of time they were shown these pictures was too short for their short term memory to hold the image in mind. Therefore, when asked if they had seen the faces before they would not recognise the image. However, when asked if they thought of an emotion when the image was flashed in front of them they would typically know the emotion demonstrated by the person in the picture. It would appear that the faster route to the emotional brain had been triggered by the facial expression.

Some call this faster reaction to emotional stimuli the emotion superhighway because of its speed of processing. Many other studies have shown how the emotions can be influenced like this in subtle ways.

Based on this we can ourselves create our own experiment to influence our subconscious emotional state.

Exercise. Creating a script for you at your best

The 7 step routine,

The following exercises have all been found, through research, to be successful in improving positive mind-state, confidence or mood. Next time you want to find yourself in a confident, motivated and positive state try doing the following first thing in the morning (before your conscious mind has fully woken up). It is best to try this for the first few times on what might be neutral days. Then when you are rehearsed try it on a more challenging day.

1. Before you get out of bed have a positive statement you utter a few times. For example, "I believe I can create my own positive mood," or "I can focus on what I need to do" or even just, "I can be confident when I need to be".

2. Have a strongly positive image of yourself from the past ready to bring to mind. In other words practice

remembering a time when you felt really good about yourself. Bring the image and the time to mind as strongly as you can.

3. Have a piece of uplifting or motivating literature that you can read.

4. Have a specific song or piece of music that has uplifting or positive connotations for you and play it as soon as possible in the morning. I find on my way to work good for this.

5. While having a shower, think through what you need to do and imagine yourself doing it with confidence and a sense of positive energy. Imagine the water in the shower bringing out the best in you, awakening in you the most positive person you can be.

6. Write down five things that you are grateful for or that you feel positive about.

7. Write down two small positive actions that you know you will do.

All of the above have been shown in different studies to have a subtle effect on people's mind-state. If you would like to read more on this kind of thing I highly recommend the book 59 Seconds by Richard Wiseman.

Exercise. Adapting self-talk

A more conscious approach is to become aware of your self-talk. Try the following,

1. **Notice what you say to yourself**. When it is negative ask yourself, "is that really true?" If it is not, say to yourself, "that is not true while that kind of thinking may have served me once it doesn't serve me now so I am letting it go".

2. **Distort that self-talk** – if the negative self-talk continues distort it by, turning down the volume, adjusting the tone - make it sound squeaky or whispered, diminish its intensity - have it fade away into the background, change its position, wherever it is located in your head shift it and push it back as far as

you can, take the emotion out of it, try saying it in a dead pan voice like the way a computer might say it. One of my favourites is to imagine someone really boring saying it in their most monotonous tone of voice. If nothing else I find this can at least get me laughing.

3. **Ask yourself -** Can I let it go? Then ask your self – will I let it go? And then finally - when will I let it go?

4. **Come up with new self-talk**. Replace the self-talk with the truth. One way of doing this is to just observe the breath. For example, "breathing in I am aware that I am breathing in, breathing out I am aware that I am breathing out."

We can also observe the emotion or the need behind the self-talk: "Breathing in I am aware of frustration, breathing out I am aware of frustration." This can serve to differentiate us from the emotion we are feeling.

I also sometimes find it helpful to just observe or notice the emotions going on, not trying to do anything with the feeling just observing its presence.

Courage and compassion

By being assertive we try to gain a balance between compassion for the other person and the strength to state our own needs. See figure below.

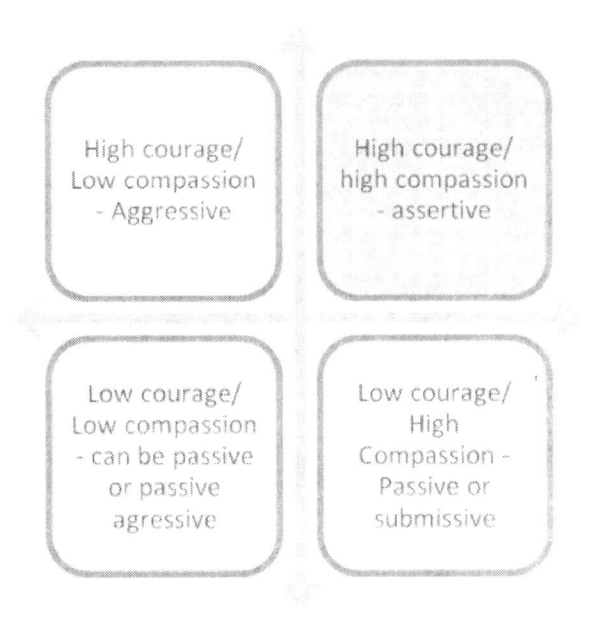

High courage/ Low compassion - Aggressive	High courage/ high compassion - assertive
Low courage/ Low compassion - can be passive or passive agressive	Low courage/ High Compassion - Passive or submissive

Asking for what we need

Being assertive and setting clear boundaries means that we get some clarity in our mind about the following:

How we feel. What we need. What we want. What we expect of another.

Having this clarity can then help us to know what and how to communicate. However, just because we know these things does not mean we must communicate them. There are times where our insight into the needs of others may lead us to choose to subjugate our own needs and put the needs of the other first at that moment. I personally believe that this is assertive if it is a conscious choice as distinct from an unconscious default pattern.

Letting go

The ultimate in self-confidence can be the ability to let go. What I mean by this is that we genuinely let go of the need to have our expectations met and the need to be in control. This is tough because it could mean considerable discomfort. It means not knowing what's next. It means asking for what we want while accepting we may never get it. It means trusting in our own ability to cope with whatever life has to offer.

Many people confuse letting go with blocking out. They look for their needs to be met or they state an expectation and when it is not met they cannot cope with the loss of control they feel so they push away the offending obstacle and block it from consciousness.

To cut someone off is not to let go it is to cut someone off. Real letting go is the ability to allow someone else be who they truly are and still be able to be around them. It is letting go of expectations or letting go of our need for them to be a certain way based on our interpretation of how things should be.

The blocking out is what usually gives rise to conflict. We ask for something that someone else cannot or will not give, despite this we think they "should" give it, then because they refuse we attempt to obliterate them from our mind. "Because you did not give me what I want or need I cannot be in your presence anymore."

Genuine assertive confidence means asking and then accepting the response. In some cases it makes sense to ask again and again but at a certain stage we need to let go and accept that this person at this time will not fulfil this need for us. In a business context this may mean taking a different action and may mean consequences for you or the other person. In a personal context it may mean just accepting what we cannot change.

Assertive or aggressive

To be confidently assertive we need to accept that people often interpret assertiveness as aggressiveness. This means we will often get a negative response to our efforts at being assertive. If we can accept that a negative response is a fairly natural response then we have moved a step closer to true assertiveness. Often people try assertive communication in conflict situations, it doesn't work for them the first time, they then cannot let go of their need to have their assertion responded to "the right way" so they begin to try aggression. This aggression usually emerges in the form of violence or silence. The violence is usually verbal and the silence is usually cutting off.

Exercise: The next time you try an assertive response in a difficult situation and you do not get what you want ask yourself these questions.

Do I feel the pull to attack or block out?
What do I need right now to remain strong and compassionate with myself and this person?
What do I need to do to remain assertive?

Can I listen a little more, reflect a little more, understand a little more, let go a little more? Can I understand better my intention and theirs?

The following is more ideal than real but it may help in focusing the mind on what you need to strengthen.

Profile of a highly assertive person.

Beliefs and mind-set.
- Believes in their own rights and the rights of others.
- Is aware of their own needs, values and highest priorities.
- Talks to themselves positively & supportively.
- Believes in the potential for win/win solutions.
- Thinks in terms of possibilities so as to break through problems.
- Creatively imagines positive outcomes.
- Values and appreciates differences in others.
- Avoids thinking the worst and tries to think the best of others.
- Avoids seeing themselves as being victimized.
- Accepts him/herself.
- Accepts responsibility.
- Chooses when to use assertion skills.

Behaviour

- Listens with empathy and clarifies understanding.
- Focuses on issues and needs rather than personalities and positions.
- Operates on what they can influence.
- Communicates clear expectations and intentions.
- Gives timely and constructive feedback.
- Attempts to understand the needs and values of others.
- Treats others with respect by using non-aggressive but assertive language.
- Avoids dominating discussions and makes their thoughts and feelings clear.
- Avoids beating around the bush.
- Seeks solutions to problems.

Results

- Develops stronger and more genuine relationships.
- Is looked on as a role model by others.
- Is seen as someone who is a positive influence.
- Is seen as someone who will bring energy, enthusiasm and positive contributions.
- Is a catalyst for positive change.
- Feels less frustration.
- Is more likely to get their needs met.
- Is more likely to achieve positive outcomes in negotiation and conflict situations.

I repeat the above is an ideal and it would be rare to meet someone with all of these qualities but there is no harm in having an aspirational ideal to work towards.

I have found it very useful to pick role models of assertiveness down through the years but I have never met any one person that will have all of the qualities one might want. It is also worth noting that most people in most situations don't want to hear assertive messages. Even for the very mature person they will usually involve some cognitive dissonance or internal upset.

Further exercises for developing assertiveness

Positive affirmation

Determine when you need to be assertive. Visualize your ideal posture and inner body state. Bring to mind and body how you feel when you are confident and feeling strong. Hear in your mind a song or piece of music that inspires you or alternatively imaginge the sound of the ocean.

Then decide on one or two statements to affirm yourself, for example,

 "I am strong and confident and able to speak my mind",

"I am able to remain calm and to think clearly

about what I need to say",

"While I may feel a little nervous I can still be assertive",

"I can put myself first when I need to".

Practice visualizing yourself in a confident assertive state and repeat the affirmation regularly especially when you need to be assertive.

Listening and reflecting

When you need to calm down, go into listening mode and reflect back what you have heard. Then think about what you need to say.

3 part assertive message

1. State the issue, behaviour or problem.

2. State the impact it has on you.

3. State what you want or need or expect.

Example, *"This soup is cold, I am not happy with it, can you bring me a fresh bowl of hot soup please."*

Example, *"You are shouting in order to get your message across. I don't like being shouted at. Could you lower your voice please."*

Joint problem solving

When you have an interpersonal issue that may be challenging suggest that you would like to brainstorm some possible alternatives or other solutions.

Broken record

This is useful in occasional situations where you need to stand your ground. The broken record is when you repeat your need until the other person shows that they have heard and understood.

For example when bringing back a faulty item to a shop and you believe you are entitled to a new item or a replacement you might continually state your entitlement, i.e. *"I am entitled to my money back or a replacement according to your customer charter"*

Focus on the problem, not the person

People will often try to make you the problem or vice versa. Instead we should avoid making generalisations about others and focus on specific problem behaviour, needs or desired results.

Understanding intent

Most people, most of the time, have a positive intent. Trying to understand the intentions of others can help us to empathise. However, do not confuse empathy with agreement. We can say and show that we understand someone without agreeing.

Stick with current issues – avoid digging up the past

During conflict there is often the risk of opening old wounds and revisiting old patterns of interaction. Always focus your efforts and energy on the current problem.

Avoid generalisations and negative affirmations

"Here we go again"

"This is always happening to me"

"No-one ever listens to my suggestions"

"They are always treating me this way"

"I'm useless in these types of situations"

"I always become nervous in interviews"

"You never listen to me"

Receiving Criticism

To become more assertive it is important to learn how to receive criticism effectively. It begins with your attitude to criticism in general. If you see criticism as something negative then it is likely to always be a problem. If on the other hand you see criticism as just feedback neither negative nor positive then you are less likely to become defensive. Again the CUBES acronym can be useful here.

Listen to the criticism. If it is generalised, like, "You're not that great at this", look for the person to be more specific.

Ask yourself is the criticism,

Credible – Does it come from a credible source, does it seem believable?

Useful – Is the criticism going to serve you personally or in the context of what you do?

Behavioural – Is it based on actual behaviour or is someone presuming to know your thoughts?

Example/evidence – Can you get an example

of the behaviour or actions to which the person is referring? Can you get some observable evidence?

Specific – Can you make the example as specific as possible so that you know exactly whether you want to change it?

If the criticism is not any of these things you need to consider getting more information or just letting it go.

***

Assertively dealing with conflict

When thinking about your approach to conflict it is worth becoming aware of your personal default approach or conflict pattern.

Most of us have a pattern when conflict arises. This pattern is usually laid down early in life. The pattern is rarely conscious and we often aren't aware of it until we learn to consciously start noticing our conflict triggers and responses.

These patterns can vary considerably but common ones are to raise the loudness and tone of the voice, become silent, become defensive, become offensive, to generalize about the problem (e.g. you're always putting me down) etc.

Exercise: Think about the last time you experienced conflict. What was your immediate response? How did this show on your face and through your words and actions? What feelings were you experiencing at the time? What was the impact of these response on you and on the other person?

Here are seven common ways of approaching conflict see if you can recognise which ones you tend to use.

7 Cs of negotiation and conflict resolution

Commercialising

The commercialising style focuses primarily on business and transactions. The mind-set is rational and business like with a focus on data, facts, figures, the bottom line and give and take. When using this style we tend to focus on what is a logically sound deal and interactions tend to be very transactional. While this style may seem like the one to use all of the time in business it makes for very cold or superficial relationships and may lack the warmth and consideration to build long term relationships particularly in the service industry. In personal situations it usually means we feel that if someone does something for us we have to do something in return and of course if we do something for someone that they then owe us a little. The term, "brownie points" is often used and internally a person using this style is often carrying out a series of checks and balances in their head. However anyone that has to take care of a person who is seriously ill or dying will know how this style doesn't always add up in the real world of relationships. Often the person trapped in this style can end up losing friends and family because they never quite live up to their standards. This is usually because most who are stuck with this mind-set don't tend to communicate their needs. They want people to intuit what those needs are.

Competing

The focus of the competing approach is to win or to beat others. When this style is used we see negotiations and conflict as games to be played or battles to be won. People who use this approach tend to place their needs above the needs of others and will use a variety of tactics to turn the situation in their favor.

Because with this style we are usually more concerned with winning the fight than finding the best solution, it can be perceived as aggressive. This may be a worthwhile approach in short term transactions but if we need to build a long term relationship this style is not likely to be very effective.

Compromising

The compromising style tends to look for a middle ground where both sides get something out of the deal. When the compromising style is used the more assertive of the two parties will sometimes end up with more.

Because compromising usually means making concessions it often sets a precedent for future negotiations and can make it difficult to get to win-win in any future interactions. Therefore this style should also be used only in short term relationships or transactions or when there is limited time to come to a better solution.

Capitulating

This style corresponds with a submissive stance. We do not want to offend, lose approval or step out of our comfort zone so we let the other side win or do it their way. This is essential if the other side holds all the power (for instance if we are in front of a judge in court) but in most situations it opens the ground for being walked on in the future. That said we should choose this style if we know that we are in the wrong and we need to apologize and rebuild a relationship of trust.

Collaborating

Most people confuse the collaborative style with the compromising style. This is, however, a mistake. Collaboration is about making sure both parties have their needs and interests met.

The mind-set for collaboration is one of abundance. We try to think that we do not have the full picture until we have genuinely understood both sides' point of view and we look to find a satisfactory agreement where all are happy. Collaboration requires that we "think win-win" and that we see the other party as a partner with whom we work to define and decide on what is good for all involved. When being collaborative we become determined to approach negotiations creatively and we work hard to redefine what is possible when minds work together.

Conniving

The conniving style seems like an unlikely style in negotiations and conflict yet it is more common than one would expect. This style focuses on win-lose but if we are on the receiving end we might not know it. Often when using this style we remain guarded, keep our intentions to ourselves and look to manipulate through covert means. In difficult interactions this style looks like passive aggression and in most cases it leads to strained relationships where trust is low.

In situations where high trust is not necessary and we want to avoid any confrontation and still win we might make the choice to use this style.

Compelling

A compelling style is one that chooses a push or coercive approach in a negotiation and conflict. The person using this style will opt for convincing the other party of the benefits of their solution or service without listening or considering the needs of the other party. This style can be overwhelming for people who are unassertive and will often win with these people in the short term. However, if it is a customer they are unlikely to return because they find this style intimidating.

This style might be used in situations where we hold more bargaining power and we want to push for a quick short term solution. However, we should be aware that the other party very often comes away feeling bruised.

Exercise: Managing self in conflict situations

Identify a situation where you experienced difficulty managing conflict (or lack of assertiveness).

How would you describe yourself in that situation?

Which of the above approaches did you use?

What feelings were underneath the above description?

Were there any other feelings underneath or alongside the feeling described above?

What need or want was behind the feeling? The list below may help,

- Need for control

- Need for security
- Need for approval
- Need for attachment or belonging
- Need for freedom
- Need for acceptance
- Need for (other).......

If you were to make an "I" statement to yourself stating what you feel and need what would that be?

What do you need to affirm to yourself when placed in this situation again?

For example, "Even though I feel .... and need ....right now I have a right to ....and I can be assertive in this situation".

Or "Even though I am feeling ....and I need .... I can listen, understand and state clearly what I need".

Below is a method of conflict resolution which will generally be useful in situations where people want to move towards a solution.

8 Steps to Conflict Resolution

Step 1. Pause and think. Take a breath and if you need to, take another one. Get into the gap between stimulus and response. Have you ever had an argument and said something you wish you hadn't. The funny thing is we usually don't gain that awareness until after the fact. If you can pause long enough you can train yourself to calm the impulsive side of the emotional brain and start engaging the rational brain and the more compassionate side of the emotional brain.

What is necessary for more mature conflict resolution is that we take responsibility for ourselves and show consideration for others. That means thinking about what we say and not just rushing in with whatever egocentric thing that comes into our heads.

Step 2. Develop an equal rights mind-set. An equal rights mind-set is one where you genuinely believe your rights and the other person's rights should have equal opportunity to be expressed. "My needs are important and so are yours." It means believing that there is always a potential for mutual gain or as they say in Transactional Analysis – "I'm OK – You're OK"

Step 3. Listen actively and flex your empathy muscles. It is not easy to listen or empathise when we experience conflict because our emotional triggers are usually screaming at us – "fight, fight, fight" or "flee, flee, flee" or "freeze, freeze, freeze".

That is why it is important to do step 1 – pause and think. Those initial deep breaths can be a lifesaver, if not a lifesaver then at least a love-saver. Because the conflict in this moment is usually not what we are reacting to, we are often reacting to years of conflict and it is not always the person we are with that was the historical subject of the earlier conflicts.

Just to summarise listen actively means, listening so as to understand not win the argument and demonstrating to the other person that you are at least trying to see their point of view. This is usually done by reflecting back to them your understanding of their perspective, opinion, view-point.

4. State your issues, intentions and needs without provocation. In other words, "this is the problem as I see it and this is what I need."

William Ury puts it very well in his book "Getting Past No",

The standard mind-set is either/or. Either you are right or your opponent (sic) is. The alternative mind-set is both/and. He (sic) can be right in terms of his experience, and you can be right in terms of yours. You can say to him: "I can see why you feel the way you do. It's entirely reasonable in terms of the experience you have had. My experience, however, has been different." You can acknowledge his view and, without challenging it, express a contrary one.

5. Focus on the problem at hand. Resist the urge to bring up the history of all of your problems with this person or to list off all of their character flaws.

Sometimes when we are offended by someone's actions towards us our mind then starts to make a list of all of the past sins committed by this person. We then begin to see what a "real ogre" they are, how selfish they are and how much they only care about themselves etc., etc. Now is the time to set the record straight, find justice and maybe even a little revenge. This is really when we have become victims, lost control and disempowered ourselves. We have allowed this present moment discomfort to become the summary of the relationship forgetting about all of the other facets. Our mental focus in that moment usually has the depth and breadth of a pinhead. We can only see the pin prick and see nothing of any of the positive aspects of the pin its uses in that moment are over shadowed by the pain we are experiencing.

Well if you find yourself in this trap (and believe me I have been there many a time) the problem is less about the other person and more about you. You most likely need to take a long pause or time out and take the time to let go of some of that baggage in the form of resentment that you have been letting stew.

I recommend some free writing – dumping all those feelings onto a page or two. This can really help to purge some of that stuff from your psyche. Alternatively talking it out with a counsellor can also help.

Step 6. Both parties write down the problem at hand. People seem to find it hard to do this but the benefits far out-weigh the dangers in my opinion. Writing down the problem helps put it out there. It makes it more objective and less subjective, less of a problem between you and me and more just a problem that needs to be solved. If possible both people should write it down in their own words. This can really help mutual understanding.

Step 7. Joint brainstorming. Write down as many solutions as you can think of – but have a rule that each person must have at least three or four ideas. At first it is good not to talk just write, then after a while read through the ideas and try to build on them. When you have done this see if you can jointly come to a decision on what action needs to be taken. If you cannot come to a decision agree to take a break and come back to it.

Step 8. Take action and review progress. It is all pointless if you are not willing to take action and do the behaviour that needs to be done.

If you come away and the other person is the only one with things to do then it is unlikely it will work. I love the quote from Stephen Covey, "if you think the problem is out there then that very thought is the problem".

Exercise: Identify an argument that you had in the past. Write down a brief description of what you can remember. Now go through each of the above steps and ask yourself what specifically you would do and say if you were to go through the conflict situation again.

Chapter 6

Manage Your Firewall

"A firewall is a device or set of devices designed to permit or deny network transmissions based upon a set of rules and is frequently used to protect networks from unauthorized access while permitting legitimate communications to pass."

From Wikipedia, the free encyclopedia

"Some stuff we let in and some stuff we just bin other stuff we don't even see because my mind says it's a sin."

Unknown

Think of any person you know reasonably well. Now ask yourself, how well they really know you. Do they sometimes make assumptions, take you for granted, judge you, criticize you. It happens to the best of us. Our minds have to learn to discriminate and so when we are young we learn to differentiate right from wrong, light from dark, "good music" from "rap" (sorry I meant "crap") etc.

However if we grow up and I mean really grow up we eventually learn that much of our differentiation is actually a form of discrimination. We make judgments based on rather crude algorithms. We think we have a picture of a person's personality, what they are like, what they are not like. Yet time and again I come across spouses who claim their partners don't know what they like, employees that say their boss doesn't understand them, customers who say they are not listened to, end users that complain about the complexity of software and people who claim to know me that really don't – nor I them for that matter.

The challenge lies in the firewall we have put up over time either to protect ourselves or just through lack of interest or motivation to genuinely attempt to truly understand another person.

The firewall can sometimes block almost everything. For example, that person you know whom you just cannot stand and no matter what they do, you do not think you can ever like them. That brand of product you had a bad experience with once or twice and now avoid at all costs, or that member of your team who you made your mind up about and nothing is going to change it. That quality your brother, sister, mother, father son, daughter has that you just can't seem to see beyond sometimes.

Well something can change it – you. I once decided to turn off all security and firewalls on my home computer. You want to know what happened? Nothing. No crash, no virus, no trojans. Also no constant messages about my security status and the computer seemed to run faster. I guess it was discriminating a bit less. It's a scary notion isn't it to actually let everything in. (N.B. I am not recommending you take this action with your own computer, I am told I was just lucky so maybe best to be safe)

I am thankful to my Mother for introducing me to a spiritual writer/philosopher called Anthony DeMello. I remember him in one of his books suggesting that we try practising non-judgement for ten minutes. Even this proved virtually impossible for me at the time (not sure if I am better at now).

Now don't get me wrong I am not suggesting that we become gullible fools. There is a slight paradox here, we need to have clear and effective boundaries but we also need to be able to let people in so as to build healthy relationships.

Most of us are aware of the personal firewalls we put up to fend others off. Likewise we are usually aware of the fact that those same firewalls do not bring out the best in the people with whom we interact.

What I am suggesting here is that we soften the boundaries from time to time. That we work on accepting people with non-judgment; that we make space for a little genuine intimacy. In a world where relationships are becoming multiplied, in some cases exponentially, in number but reduced in physical and emotional presence people's need for belonging and intimacy is likely to get more and more neglected. I love the internet and I even think Facebook is a wonderful invention but I see none of them as substitutes for personal presence.

When we allow intimacy we are allowing communication to happen at a deeper level. It usually involves opening our hearts to someone and expressing our vulnerability and shared humanity. Of course this is why it's scary; the danger in opening up and allowing people in is that we will get hurt. I think people are so scared of this that they will often develop a mask of cynicism that breaks down any attempt or move towards closeness or connection.

Growing up in my own family the layer of cynicism became so thick that I once wore it with pride, thinking that it was a healthy thing to view the world through such a warped lens and not realizing how much it put people off. I still battle with this side of myself to this day.

Exercise. Softening the firewall

The next time you get a chance to listen to someone after you have put down this book try to practice taking a few bricks away from the firewall.

If the person is someone you know, try to see them afresh, seeing the person here now, not the person whom you know from history. Try to listen, really listen with acceptance and a little less evaluation and judgement.

There is a fear in doing this. The fear, I believe, is that to do this is to enter into the unknown. It is easier to keep up the firewall and filter things through the screen of the world we already know. To do otherwise is like entering into dark territory, uncharted land. But therein lies the wonder, for it can mean experiencing something completely new. For the other person it can feel as if you are there, present, attending, listening and acknowledging their presence.

When another person attends, listens, sees us and accepts us for who we are we often feel as if our very existence has been acknowledged. This in turn may lessen the loneliness or sense of isolation that we all feel from time to time.

When to raise the firewall

Of course there will be people and situations where you find it hard to manage your emotions effectively. Some people at certain stages of their lives can demonstrate a lot of toxic emotions and occasionally you might come across people who always have a toxic effect on you.

Not all of us are affected by the same people, in the same way and to the same extent. However, with some people we may need to raise the firewall so as to inoculate ourselves from time to time. If we cannot learn to do this then that person can have an unhealthy effect on us.

One of the first things to acknowledge when you feel the toxic effects of another is that their stuff is not your stuff and that you cannot control their stuff.

Secondly you need to acknowledge that your level of conscious control over your own reaction to them needs to increase. In other words you need to begin self-management strategies. Here are a few examples of firewall self-management strategies when with toxic people or in toxic situations.

1. Affirm yourself – "I am aware of ……..(the emotion you feel) and I am OK."

2. Focus on your breath and ground yourself – "Breathing in I am aware of my breath, breathing out I feel solid like a mountain or a rock." Or, "breathing in I am grounded, breathing out I am relaxing."

3. Visualize I strong inner state. Bring back a memory of a time when you felt strong, stable and able to face anything.

Act as if you feel like that right now.

4. Imagine that your firewall is like a strong, firm and flexible force field against which any toxic emotion just bounces or at its worst only trickles in a tiny little bit.

5. If the toxic effects are getting through your defenses it may not be a good time to employ empathy it may be a time for you to protect yourself.

6. On some occasions you may need to remove yourself physically from the sitatuion so that you can work on building your firewall and making it stronger.

The danger of not managing your firewall is either that you become so stressed or anxious in response to the other person that it causes you health problems or that you strike out with words or body in an effort to control the threat. The key is to realize that it is your inability to take responsibility for your own reactions to others' emotions that is the bigger threat than others' emotions. The problem is in trying to influence another when they are most likely least open to influence and their effect on us is rendering us at our least influential. People who have tantrums rarely if ever have a positive influences but people who respond to them with tantrums or something similar have just as little positive influence. Sometimes it makes sense to stand your ground and choose an assertive response to others negative stuff but sometimes it also makes sense to raise your guard or even to run away and fight (or respond more healthily) another day.

Chapter 7

Value Differences

"I put all my genius into my life; I put only my talent into my works".

Oscar Wilde

"Success is achieved by developing our strengths, not by eliminating our weaknesses."

Marilyn Vos Savant

I used to have a prejudice against personality theories. I believed that you could not and should not box people into a type or limited set of behaviours. A trait that is probably indicative of my personality type, no doubt. However, what I now realise is that I was boxing the concept in and limiting its scope. Understanding personality is not necessarily limiting and in fact can be quite liberating. It is not to say that we are all this or all that, it is simply suggesting that we all tend to have preferences when it comes to behaviour, mental processing and interacting with our world.

Most people have a preference for their right or left hand when writing. My eldest son is left handed but he prefers to kick a ball with his right foot. I am right handed but when I play guitar I fret the chords on the neck of the guitar with my left hand. After more than 30 years of doing this I find it virtually impossible to do it the other way. My left hand has been well trained to do one thing and my right another.

I make this point to show that our personality style is similar, we all have preferences but that is not to say that we cannot learn new behaviours or thinking more associated with a non-preferred personality type. I know plenty of introverts for example who demonstrate lots of extrovert behaviour in certain contexts.

One of the simplest and most accessible models of personality is DISC. The theory behind DISC was first suggested by William

Moulton Marsden but it draws on many different theories in psychology and a number of four factor models of personality have been posited over the last 80 years or so.

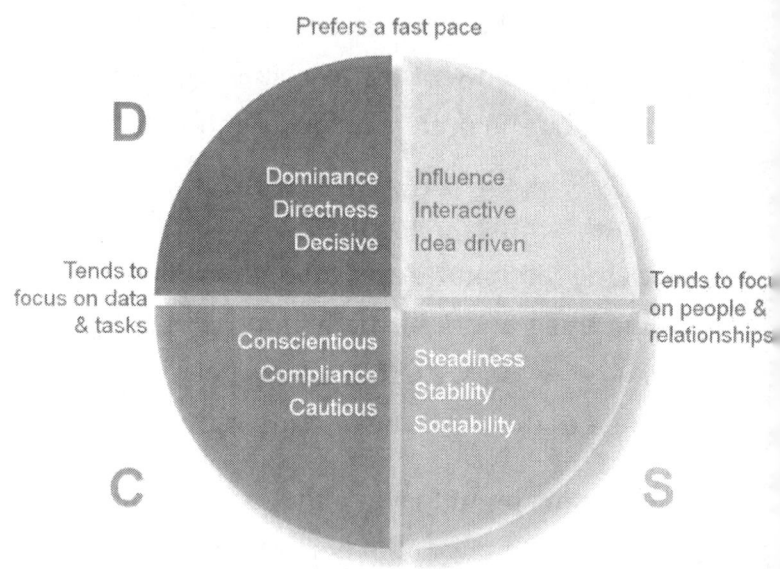

Prefers a fast pace

D

Dominance
Directness
Decisive

I

Influence
Interactive
Idea driven

Tends to focus on data & tasks

Tends to focus on people & relationships

Conscientious
Compliance
Cautious

Steadiness
Stability
Sociability

C

S

Prefers a slower, steady pace

Below is a brief introduction to the four areas of DISC. From the information provided you can probably get a sense of where your preferences lie but it is worth keeping in mind that we all show certain amounts from each of the four principal areas.

The D preference – Dominant, directive, driven : A high D score usually indicates a person who likes to focus on getting results as soon as possible. This person shows a strong need to be in control and to direct operations. A high D will usually be strong willed and assertive with a significant focus on the task and technical aspects of work, as opposed to the relational and
emotive aspects. People with high D scores achieve influence by making a difference to desired results or the bottom line. They can sometimes be too aggressive however and care is required that they do not leave others behind when achieving their goals.

Words to describe a strong "D" style,
- Dominant
- Direct
- Decisive
- Driven
- Demanding
- Determined
- Self-assured
- Self-motivated
- Pushy
- Impatient
- Ambitious

- Commanding
- Results orientated
- Quick acting

The I preference – Influencing, imaginative, initiating: A high "I" score usually indicates a "people" orientation with a quick approach to getting tasks done. People who are predominantly "I" are often full of ideas about how to achieve things. They are often great at starting new projects, however finishing them may be an issue at times. Because the "I" style can be a bit flighty, focus and concentrating efforts can often be a challenge. "I"s are often quite expressive, engaging and empathetic. While they often express high ideals and principles, keeping to these ideals can be a challenge for them. They can be quick to see breach of these ideals in others but often miss the same fault in themselves. Because "I"s seek to impress others they are often good at inspiring and influencing.

Words to describe a strong "I" style,
- Imaginative
- Idealistic
- Initiating
- Influencing
- Impulsive

- Inspirational
- Creative
- Playful
- Expressive
- Talkative
- Unfocused
- Agitated
- Disorganised
- Flighty

The "S" preference – Sociable, supportive, sensitive: People who score very high in the "S" dimension will have a relationship orientation and an evenly paced approach to getting things done. The "S" is often motivated to seek harmony in groups and this can have a calming influence in teams. High "S" people will tend to have a deliberate and steady approach to what they do and while they can often resist change once bought into the change they will be the ones who will take it to completion.

They like to take a project from start to finish. They like time for preparation and planning and do not like to be pushed to meet urgent deadlines. It is in their nature to be sensitive to the emotions and needs of others, so they can find it difficult to be assertive.

Words to describe a strong "S" style,

- Sociable
- Steady
- Supportive
- Sensitive
- Stubborn
- Empathetic
- Agreeable
- Trusting
- Accepting
- Dependable
- Unassertive
- Easy going
- Indecisive
- Inhibited

The "C" preference – Conscientious, cautious, cognitive: Strong and steady task orientation is usually an indicator of a high "C" style. If this style is very high scoring the person can come across as aloof or stand offish. They like to work on things that involve data, facts and logic.

People with a "C" style will be careful, cautious

and detail oriented, their goal is to produce quality output that will have an impact on results. They like to get into the detailed analysis of things and tasks and understand how they work and what will make them work better. People with a high "C" style can come across as uncaring because they are less expressive than others. However, they usually care quite deeply and so principles and values can be very important to them, in some cases so important that they will take a strong stand to achieve what is right.

Words to describe a strong "C" style,
- Cautious
- Conscientious
- Cognitive
- Compliant
- Careful
- Precise
- Analytical
- Organised
- Systematic
- Unsociable
- Perfectionistic
- Self-contained
- Evaluative

Bringing out the best in each style

The "D" style preference– dominance, directness, decisiveness

When interacting or working with a D style provide plenty of opportunity to succeed. Be direct and forthright; tell it like it is, they will respect you for this.

Be careful not to assume that they know just because they appear to be confident. If you are teaching them or delegating to them take time to understand and question them to ensure that they have got what they need. This applies to the person being delegated to in work or the child who is packing their rucksack going on a hike.

As soon as possible allow them to take control and or take initiative but again be careful, do not do this too soon otherwise they may crash and burn due to the fact that their competence had not yet been fully developed.

When communicating with a high "D" avoid looking for lots of detail. They want to get to work as soon as possible so if you know the fastest, cheapest, best, way to do something, don't be afraid to just tell them.

If you know the person with the "D" style well, you trust their character and they have developed a high level of competence, give them a desired outcome or goal and let them get the results their way. You do not have to spend a lot of time praising them as they typically will know what a good result looks like, however, do acknowledge their success when they do succeed.

If you want to bring out the best in the "D" style be sure not to let them get stuck in a job with little chance for progress or a lot of routine, detail focused work.

The high "D" will always be looking for the next challenge and how they can win over any obstacles their environment produces for them. Be sure not to let yourself become one of those obstacles as a temperamental "D" can behave like a bull in a china shop if someone gets in their way without good reason.

Always try to remember "D"s want to get results now so don't beat around the bush.

Bringing out the best in the "I" style – influencing, imagination, initiating.

The basic intention behind the I style is to either influence or gain approval, so first and foremost it is important to acknowledge them and give them plenty of attention and praise.

Allow lots of opportunities for this person to be creative and to use the many ideas that they tend to come up with. Because high "I"s tend to come up with a lot of ideas we can sometimes find it intimidating to be around them so be careful not to deflate them by knocking their ideas or dismissing them as irrelevant.

It can be difficult to find a balance with the "I" as they need opportunities to create and inspire but they also very often need to be grounded and to find focus.

Surprisingly, however, they can often get a lot more done than one would imagine. If we can coach them effectively so that their inspirational side is given a voice and they get to execute effectively and reap the rewards of an idea brought to its conclusion we will see how the "I" can truly shine.

It is important to avoid giving the high "I" a lot of mundane tasks and too much detail or repetition. However, like the high "D" you need to be sure that they get the message when communicating with them so sometimes asking an "I" to summarise in a work situation can be effective.

Try to be open to the spontaneity and creativity of the high "I" but also help them to contain it when necessary.

Set clear guidelines with them and be sure to identify what the absolute priorities of a task or project are. Observe and attend to their efforts and use warm and open body language with them. Look for ideas from them but be careful, they will often find it hard to say no when you look for their help. Hence, the person with the I style, because they have a deep-rooted need to influence and seek approval, can often end up taking on too much and not taking good enough care of their own highest priorities. This applies particularly to their personal needs.

High "I"s can become martyrs to their own cause sometimes believing they are solving the world's problems while not realising that they are causing more harm than good. Also when others don't realise the great works they are achieving they can sometimes harbour resentment and internalise anger. Providing courageous compassionate feedback can be very important for the high "I".

Bringing out the best in the "S" style – steadiness, stability, sociability.

Because the "S" seeks harmony they can find it difficult sometimes to be assertive but when pushed they can become quite stubborn about issues that are important to them.

If given a chance the high "S" can have a stabilising and harmonising effect on work and in groups. Because of their need for harmony it is important to take time to build rapport with them. Give clear expectations, clear boundaries and plenty of time where work is concerned. The "S" style likes to work at a steady pace and in a fairly systematic way.

When working with the "S" it is important to understand any problems or concerns they have as these can often niggle at them causing them to worry or get anxious.

Be sure and stay in contact with the "S" and let them know you care about them and their contribution. Work at maintaining a warm, friendly and supportive approach when relating to them. Be prepared to give a significant amount of detail and to observe and give feedback particularly in the early stages of a project. Eventually, however, you may need to give a gentle push so that they let go and begin to work on their own initiative. Push too soon however and they will often feel threatened or insecure. For the "S" style it can be a thin line between their stretch zone and their comfort zone.

If you work with the "S" style to build a good supportive structure around them they will show steady results, provide a harmonising effect and likely be one of your most reliable friends, workers or teammates.

Bringing out the best in the "C" style - Conscientious, cautious, cognitive.

The intention of the "C" style is to achieve quality results. With quality being the key word here.

The "C" style will operate at their best when given time to focus on a task that requires a detail orientation, a quality output that does not involve significant risk or a need for them to be highly creative. Typically they would prefer to work alone and data, logic and systems are often their preferred domains. Hence, many accountants, engineers, scientists and, I.T. people are high scorers when it comes to the "C" style.

The "C" wants to be given clear and precise expectations and instructions. They like a well thought out process that is risk-free. If there is high risk they will often be the first to point it out. If a "C" is experienced they would like to design the process themselves, however, they will often be the first to tell you that they do not have the level of experience required.

Sometimes the difficulty with a "C" style is getting them to design a process that someone other than they themselves will understand (this probably explains why for many years end users were so challenged with some computer programmes).

The key is to be clear about what you want, the standard you want and the way you want something delivered. Be prepared however to explain why or have data or evidence to back up your logic. From time to time you will need to encourage them to come out of the detail and take a helicopter view and to connect with people on whom their work has an impact.

The high "C" will often need help knowing when to let go of the detail and when a job is good enough. Because of this coaching in regard to balancing the priorities of getting results on time and getting quality results will often be required.

Very often "C"s will not automatically volunteer information and so if we need to know what's going on with them we need to ask questions so as to understand their mind-set, their values or their needs.

Emotional stability\Neuroticism - another personality trait.

DISC does not account for neuroticism or emotional stability. The reason for this, perhaps, is that disc is primarily used in the business world and very often is not administered by trained psychologists. There is, however, significant evidence that neuroticism or emotional stability exists as a separate personality trait.

The degree to which this trait is genetic or a response to our environment is less clear, however, it is most likely that our temperament is genetically influenced and then gets reinforced by our upbringing and social circumstance.

One way of thinking about neuroticism and emotional stability is to consider these and the role they play in regard to each of the DISC styles.

If we were to measure emotional stability and neuroticism with to end points on a continuum we would find that the majority of individuals fall around the centre point.

However some individuals will have higher scores on neuroticism which will mean that they tend to respond to stress with a higher intensity than most or they are more likely to have a low lying anxiety in most situations. Typically we are then likely to see the more negative aspects of their DISC style exacerbated. So "D"s will tend to be more domineering. "I"s may crave approval more.

The "S" style will withdraw where harmony is not present and "C"s will get more obsessive about order and control.

I will give a brief idea of what we are likely to see with each area of the DISC model of personality when neuroticism is high and when emotional stability is high.

The "D" style and emotional stability\neuroticism.

When someone with a strong "D" style has a high level of neuroticism they will typically come across as quite aggressive, controlling and will seek to dominate and control. Their response in stressful situations will be to try and directly control the behaviour of others often through aggressive means. The most likely emotion that will emerge will be anger and so the extreme of this will be the person who tends to blow up or rage.

On the other hand the "D" who shows a strong sense of emotional stability will harness the traits of their "D" style and contain the more negative elements. This will often result in them being clear, goal oriented, quite visionary and direct in regard to what they expect and want from others. However, they will also be aware of the impact that even normal assertiveness can have on people who tend to be more passive and so they will be more inclined to adapt their style.

The emotionally stable "D" will typically remain calm under pressure but they will show a sense of focus and urgency that will help them to get the results they need.

The emotionally stable "D" that has come under pressure will typically come across like a benevolent dictator; choosing when to dominate and direct but typically doing it for the benefit of all and showing enough consideration not to leave people falling down dead in their wake.

The "I" style and emotional stability/neuroticism.

Because approval and influence are fundamental to the "I" style, when neuroticism is high they will likely come across as either very needy or at times sycophantic. Their tendency will be to vary who they are depending on who they are with. When mistakes are made or when the "I" doesn't follow through the person with the neurotic "I" style will tend to avoid dealing with or admitting to the mistakes and may lie or come up with lots of excuses why they couldn't deliver on commitments.

High "I"s will often over explain and excuse when challenged and if they display high levels of neuroticism they will do this to the extreme, acting as if the challenge is a personal affront. The neurotic side of the "I" underneath can feel that even the smallest challenge to them is a personal affront that needs to be defended.

Another neurotic tendency of the "I" is to

harbour resentment for not being appreciated. They cannot understand how people do not see all the good work they do and as mentioned before despite quite expertly putting on a brave face, beneath the surface there can be deep feelings of resentment and anger. In some cases they themselves are not even aware of this resentment.

Because of the desire to please the "I" shies away from being assertive and so they can also burn themselves out trying to please all of the people they wish to influence.

On the other hand the more emotionally stable "I" will tend to be highly creative, inspiring and influential. Their calmer and less agitated approach to life tends to provide them with a focused energy in the areas of creativity, communication, empathy and people skills. Also because of their speed of processing they will tend to get a lot done in a short space of time. They will also show an ability to let go of past failures, rejections or let downs and move on.

The "S" style and emotional stability\neuroticism.

The "S" strives for harmony particularly where human relations are concerned. When things get pressured and stressful the "S" with a high neuroticism score will likely withdraw and go inward. It is not uncommon in this circumstance for the "S" to feel quite overwhelmed and frazzled and they may withdraw altogether or take an extremely stubborn stance. A highly neurotic "S" can be a conflicting mix of someone who wants harmony but keeps pushing people away for fear of emotional discomfort.

The more emotionally stable "S" will show a high level of emotional maturity. They will usually have a strong sense of awareness of a group's or relationship's needs and while they may not like being assertive they will push themselves to be assertive when required. While their desire for harmony is strong they are aware of times when conflict is natural and will transcend their need for harmony so as to work through the conflict.

The "C" style and emotional stability/ neuroticism.

The neurotic "C" is often lampooned in sitcoms on TV. Just think of Monica from Friends, Felix from the Odd Couple or Sheldon from The Big Bang Theory only less comedic.

Highly neurotic "C"s can get so pedantic and so detail oriented that they will find it difficult to complete a task. They will often lean towards hypochondria learning as much as they can about health, medication and side effects, food, environment and anything else that might have an impact on their personal safety. Ironically their relentless striving for organisation and control can often leave them in a world of emotional chaos.

The difference with an emotionally stable high "C" is that they will show an awareness of their need for control, compliance and risk free situations and so they will try to find a balance in their approach. Their conscientiousness will make them think carefully about decisions but their emotional stability will lead them to taking healthy risks that are ultimately for the better.

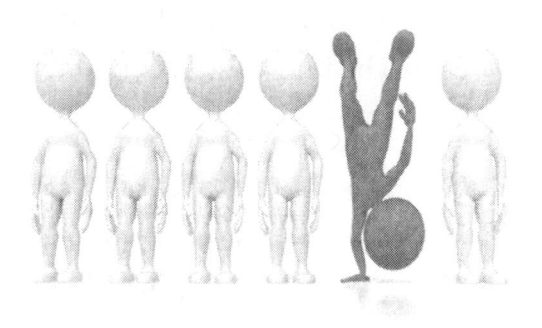

The key with understanding personal styles is simple but not easy to implement:

1. Understand the advantages and disadvantages, strengths and weaknesses of your own preference.

2. Raise your awareness over time of when it is useful to allow these preferences to guide you and when you need to transcend or rise above them; choose a different approach.

3. Get to know the preferences of others and tolerate, accept and value them for who they are. If possible align their job role to suit who

they are and again, if possible, teach them when they need to rise above their natural bent and be a little more than who they are.

That is not to say that you should let "D"s walk all over you, let "C"s drive you nuts looking for the risk in everything, allow "I"s to start 27 new projects and complete none of them or permit "S"s to disappear into the woodwork when conflict arises.

What you need to do is be aware that because they have preferences those preferences are likely to be guiding them much of the time and usually quite unconsciously.

So the high "C" is not looking for every detail to frustrate you it is to relieve possible frustration in themselves.

The high "I" is not trying to drive you nuts with their constant barrage of new ideas or striving for your approval they are often just doing what they do and love best, innovating, creating, inspiring.

The high "D" is not meaning to cut you short or be abrupt they are just trying to appease their need to get the job done.

The high "S" is not wanting to drive you nuts

with their focus on people and feelings they just see relationships and harmony as a primary goal in any situation.

***

Optimizing your strengths

An awareness of personal styles or personality is just one way of looking at our personal characteristics, traits and strengths. Marcus Buckingham and Donald Clifton introduced the strengths finder in their 2001 book Now Discover Your Strengths. The basic premise of this book is hard to disagree with. Buckingham and Clifton found in their research that when people are using or working with their strengths they are usually happier, more engaged and are more likely to perform at their best. Strengths finder identifies 32 specific strengths and can help you to identify with a fairly high level of validity what your strengths are.

However when bringing out the best in others we can't always get them to fill in a strengths finder survey so I have identified a number of key strengths here that you can identify for yourself and think about in regard to others.

Exercise: Identifying strengths and weaknesses,

From the list below identify eight areas that you are particularly good at, you may have specific strengths that are not on the list it is just a guide.

Attracting customers, accounting, auditing, adapting, administration, analyzing, arranging, budgeting, building relationships, building teams, briefing, balancing accounts, communicating, controlling, co-ordinating, creating new processes, coaching, checking work, design, decision making, doing detailed work, developing others, directing,

empathizing, encouraging others, evaluating work, examining, explaining, executing, editing, engaging others, finding resources, fixing technical problems, formulating plans, finalizing plans, guiding a team, gathering data, generating ideas, helping others succeed, hosting, ideating, implementing plans, influencing customers, influencing the team, influencing people, initiating projects, innovating, improving processes,

judging, keeping records, leading a team, learning, listening, locating, managing people, marketing, mentoring, monitoring work, motivating, negotiating, navigating, observing, organizing, persuading, planning, preparing, presenting to others, problem-solving, public speaking, politicking, questioning, qualifying,

researching, resolving disputes, reporting, recording work, repairing technical problems, rapport building, scheduling, strategizing, selling, setting up projects, supervising, teaching, team-work, trouble-shooting, training individuals, training a group, tracking, technical skills, understanding others, verbalizing, volunteering, verifying, writing reports, working on routine tasks.

What are your top five strengths?

Of this top five which ones do you engage with or enjoy doing most? Try to pick three.

In what ways can working with these strengths help or fulfil a need for others?

In what ways can these strengths offer value?

What proportion of your day is spent using the above strengths?

If you were to increase the amount of time spent using these strengths in your working day what would be the impact on you and others?

Now identify some of the areas from the list that are weaknesses or things you dislike doing that you find yourself having to do a lot.

When you work on these things how do you tend to feel?

How can you reduce or limit the amount of time spent doing these specific things?

If you manage people or are a parent or in any other kind of leadership or guidance role the next exercise may be of help.

Now consider one of the people that you work with closely or that you manage.

And go through a similar process.

What are their top five strengths?

Of these strengths which ones do you think are the most engaging for them, which ones do you think they really love doing?

At the moment what proportion of their day is spent focusing on these strengths?

Are there ways that you can help them to focus on their strengths even more?

Which specific areas do you think they dislike doing?

Are there ways that you can help them reduce or limit the amount of time focusing on their weaknesses or the things they hate doing?

Most people report feeling more engaged, happier, more confident, more energised when focusing on and using their personal strengths.

While it is not always possible to have people working with their strengths all of the time, as managers or influencers we can at least help people to move in the direction of their strengths or at least to minimize or limit the amount of time spent on their weaknesses.

I use the model below when working with coaching clients and occasionally when focusing on a business's strategy. I find when people get clear in each of the four circles their focus and engagement tends to amplify significantly. The idea is to get some clarity and alignment between your strengths, your needs, values and aspirations, where you can add value and your current capacity.

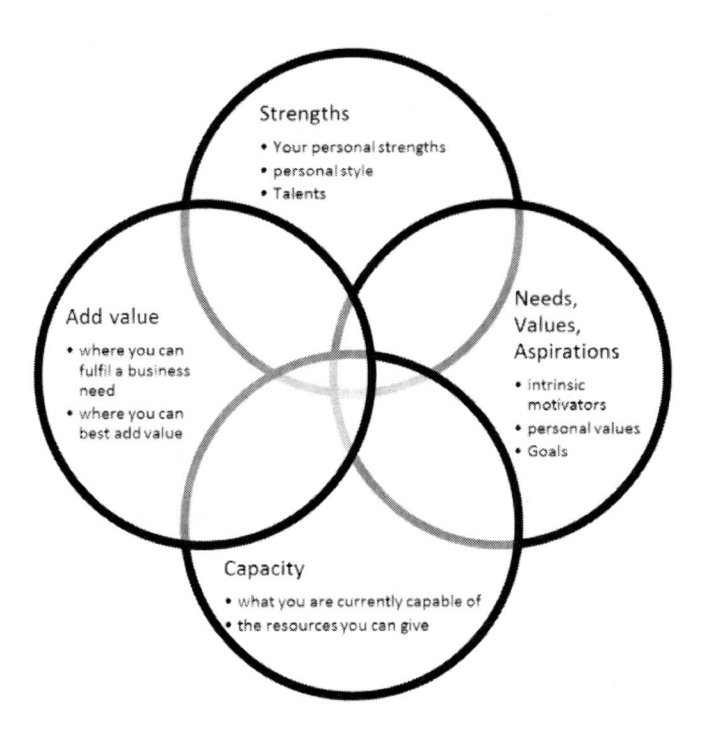

Strengths
- Your personal strengths
- personal style
- Talents

Add value
- where you can fulfil a business need
- where you can best add value

Needs, Values, Aspirations
- intrinsic motivators
- personal values
- Goals

Capacity
- what you are currently capable of
- the resources you can give

Intrinsic motivation.

Intrinsic motivation is another way to tap into people's inner strength. Intrinsic motivators are the internal drives that are typically non-tangible and that drive behaviour and contribute to the meaning of day-to-day life for most people.

There are many ways of describing intrinsic motivators and no theory fully encapsulates what exactly intrinsic motivators are or how exactly they should be labelled. I have done a meta-analysis of some of the theories of intrinsic motivation and come up with nine basic clusters that could broadly be described as intrinsic motivators.

Exercise: Look at the list of intrinsic motivators or needs below. On a scale of 1 to 10 where ten is very important and 1 is not at all important score each one in relation to how important a need it is for you.

1. Autonomy, choice, freedom
2. Achievement, challenge
3. Pride, self-esteem, recognition
4. Fun, pleasure, enjoyment
5. Connection, belonging, support
6. Creativity, self-expression
7. Art, beauty, aesthetics
8. Order, organisation, control

9. Purpose, ideals, meaningfulness

Having ranked these needs/motivators now ask yourself are there ways, at the moment, that you could satisfy them a little more? Which specific ones that are important to you have you been neglecting and which ones, if focused on a little more, might increase your current intrinsic motivation?

Now rank the intrinsic motivators in terms of a member of your work team, a child, a close friend or family member. You will of course be making an educated guess here but the purpose is to try and empathise and understand what motivates this person.

On a score of 1 to 10 how important is each of these to the person you are thinking of?

1. Autonomy, choice, freedom
2. Achievement, challenge
3. Pride, self-esteem, recognition
4. Fun, pleasure, enjoyment
5. Connection, belonging, support
6. Creativity, self-expression

7. Art, beauty, aesthetics
8. Order, organisation, control
9. Purpose, ideals, meaningfulness

Now ask yourself, are there ways that I can help this person tap into their intrinsic motivators? If you manage this person would it be worth discussing this with them?

Are there ways that you can make you're your relationship with this person more need fulfilling? If you are their manager, are there ways that you can make their job role more fulfilling or more intrinsically motivating?

If you are a manager it can be a great opportunity for building the relationship with your team, getting to know them and creating coaching situations, if you sit down with them and discuss what their intrinsic motivations within their job role are and how you can help them to make their job more fulfilling. I recommend to managers who wish to improve their coaching skills and manager employee relationship that they work on understanding the four circle coaching model above and spending time understanding intrinsic motivation better.

The ideal is to try to help somebody gain a high score in each of the four circles. If we can get a strong intersection between all four the person gets to focus on their strengths, engage in work that they value or are passionate about doing, fulfill intrinsic needs and add value to whatever business they are in.

Chapter 8

Transcending and Leading the Way

"Lead from the back — and let others believe they are in front."

Nelson Mandela

"If we could change ourselves, the tendencies in the world would also change. As a man changes his own nature, so does the attitude of the world change towards him….."

M.K. Gandhi

A participant on a leadership development programme came up to me during the programme and said that the results of her 360° feedback report are skewed because of the sample of people he chose. He also states how angry he is with some of the comments made about him that they are unjust and unfair. He asked me if he can get the names of the people who responded. I state that he cannot and I explain to him that this is still useful feedback but that he should go to the people and discuss it to learn more. He insists that there is little point as those people already have their mind made up about him and won't give him a chance.

The above incident is not that common on programmes, the majority of people are willing to accept the feedback they get and see it as a useful awareness building exercise.

Some people, however, are stuck in a world where things are being done to them. A world that is dictated more from their past experience than their personal values or future goals. They cannot understand why bad things keep happening to *them.*

At some point in our lives we begin to realise that we are responsible for ourselves. That means owning our flaws, accepting our mistakes, realising we are not special, seeing reality as it is not as we think it should be and taking responsibility for the way we choose to respond in any given circumstance.

Our genes, personality, family, school, socio-economic circumstance have all contributed to the story of who we are but they are not the sum total of who we are.

Transcending and leading requires that we accept our conditioned responses, raise our awareness of them and instead of automatically letting them happen, working at consciously choosing our response in the moment.

It is my firm belief that the more that we can find calm on a physical and emotional level the more we can employ a deeper stronger, more strategic and, dare I say it, moral path of action. This path requires that we rise above our petty egotistical inadequacies and our warped sense of who we are and what the world is and begin to see the beauty inherent in the world and the potential for greatness in most all of us. This is not easy when we are agitated and distracted half of the time by our need to satisfy our desires and appease our hunger for safety, society, love, achievement.

That is not to say that these things are not fruitful it is just that our occasional obsessions with them usually lead us to making less healthy decisions.

If to transcend means to rise above and to lead is to beat a path for others to follow then we need to cultivate physical, emotional, intellectual and moral strength required to rise above and we must at least attempt to see the path that we wish to pursue.

Many of us are too busy, distracted or engaged in the short term game to rise above and see where we truly need to go. The compulsion to satisfy external demands in the moment have often clouded our ability to see either into the future or from the perspective of another. We get lost in the thick of thin things as Stephen Covey would call it.

When we look at people who have done this; who have transcended their situation and set the example, we see them both rising above their current situation and often making an attempt at carving out direction for themselves and often others too. People like Gandhi, Nelson Mandella, Rosa Parks and Helen Keller were all examples of people caught in difficult circumstances who had to continually rise above their personality and their situation. This was often combined with a fierce determination to succeed and usually the courage to face rejection or defeat and push on through the barriers that life presented them.

This can start at a quite simple level by just noticing all of the situations that get you tangled, agitated, frustrated, stressed and ask yourself how can I rise above this and see the longer term goal. This is not as easy as it sounds but it can be done. In fact I believe it is one of the reasons why we have the function of cognitive awareness. It is there to help us adapt and optimise so as to create a situation that is ultimately more beneficial for all.

Here are a list of questions to ask yourself if you get caught in a quagmire and need to get beyond current short term thinking.

Start by taking some time out then take three to four deep breaths, relax to the best of your ability and then reflect on the following,

How can I rise above this current situation I am in and see more than what my current focus is showing me?

What is my long term goal or my highest priority at the moment?

What way do I really want to achieve this goal?

What internal barriers are blocking me now?

How can I transcend these barriers and move forward?

How can I achieve some relaxed silence for a while so as to settle my mind and focus my awareness?

What is the best thing for me to think, believe and say to myself at this time?

In addition to the above I strongly recommend taking the time out to explore your personal sense of purpose and the values that guide you moment to moment, the following reflective exercise may help with that.

Reflective exercise for exploring purpose, values and long term influence

Guidelines

Set aside a significant amount of time. Put on some peaceful music or if you are near to nature tune into the sounds around you.
Read the quotes first just to stimulate your reflection and thinking.
Allow yourself to relax, breathe deeply and become inner focused.
Read and reflect on each question and what it means to you. Allow your thoughts to flow as freely as possible.
Notice any particular images, words, feelings, voices, thoughts, memories or associations that each question brings up for you.
Begin writing your answers.
Allow your pen to flow on the page as quickly as you can without pausing or stopping to think how good or bad the answer is.

The Quotes

"I would like to be known as a person who is concerned about freedom and equality and justice and prosperity for all people."

Rosa Parks

"I learned that courage was not the absence of fear, but the triumph over it. The brave man is not he who does not feel afraid, but he who conquers that fear."

Nelson Mandela

"The most beautiful thing we can experience is the mysterious. It is the source of all true art and all science."

Albert Einstein

If the doors of perception were cleansed, everything would appear to man as it is, infinite.

William Blake

Many people suffer from the fear of finding oneself alone, and so they don't find themselves at all.

Rollo May

Your visions will become clear only when you can look into your own heart. Who looks outside, dreams; who looks inside, awakes.

C.G. Jung

"What you do makes a difference, and you have to decide what kind of difference you want to make."

Jane Goodall

Have patience with everything that remains unsolved in your heart. ...live in the question.

Rainer Maria Rilke.

The questions begin on the next page.

The Questions

Question 1. Imagine yourself looking down from above at you in your current situation. What are the most important things that you do from day to day?

Question 2. What resistances or blocks are you experiencing in relation to positively influencing others or being at your best?

Question 3. In what situations are you experiencing the following?
- self criticism
- cynicism or scepticism
- anxiety, fear or hopelessness

Question 4. In what way do the above inner qualities or voices serve you? Or how have they served you in the past?

Question 5. What can you do to let go of these voices when you need to?

Question 6. Try to describe your ideal approach to influencing others? What kind of lasting impression do you genuinely wish to leave with people?

Question 7. What more do you need to do to develop your potential to influence others in a positive way?

Question 8. What more positive or fruitful behaviours, attitudes or mind-sets do you want to develop over the next few years?

Question 9. What do you want your friends, family, direct reports and colleagues to say about you when they move on to their next stage or position or when they talk about you in ten to twenty years' time? What would you like them to have learned from you as an individual/colleague/leader?

Question 10. What aspects of yourself do you need to learn to accept gracefully?

Finish these statements

"When it comes to having an influence in the world or on others I see my overall purpose, mission or intention as being……………..

The most obvious belief about influencing others that I need to let go of is……

The most obvious belief about influencing others that I need to take on is……..

The most obvious behaviour that I need to reduce or stop doing so as to be more of a positive influence is…..

If I let go of this the impact is likely to be …….
The most obvious behaviour that I need to start doing or start doing more often so as to be a positive influence is…..

If I do this the impact is likely to be …….

Identify two small behaviours that would bring you closer to being a more positive influence.

Write down one medium term goal that will help you in becoming a more positive influence that you can focus on achieving right now.

Chapter 9

The Whole Symphony

"My soul is a hidden orchestra; I know not what instruments, what fiddle strings and harps, drums and tamboura I sound and clash inside myself. All I hear is the symphony."

Fernando Pessoa

"Apparently there is nothing that cannot happen today." –

Mark Twain

You only live once, but if you do it right, once is enough."

Mae West

I started out my working life as a musician. To this day I still enjoy playing music and even writing an occasional song. There is something about what music does for the soul, whether it is just listening and enjoying a symphony or song, playing with other musicians or hearing a song I wrote recorded for the first time. Music seems to encapsulate much of what is positive about life both physically, mentally, emotionally and metaphorically.

When we choose to listen to the music of another we contribute to the harmony or resonance of human life. We realise that every person is not one note or one beat. Nor are they one song sung over and over. Each and every one of us is like a symphony or a song cycle. Yes some of the movements are more passionate and some are easier to listen to. Some parts sound as if they are barely there and others reach an incredible crescendo that seems to get our heart beating faster. We find some music more accessible than others. Other types of music can be more difficult and dissonant yet many people like that too. Every day new forms of music emerge from the combination of usually just twelve notes put together in some form of rhythm and melody.

One thing is for sure the music is always moving, changing, the melody evolving and the sense of time rising and falling. There are musicians who play mostly for themselves and musicians who love to just entertain; either way the passion for music is still there.

For me, I find the wonderful thing about a new piece of music is the sense of not knowing where it may go next. Although I do like to be surprised, I don't like to be totally shocked when hearing music. That said I know people who love to be shocked. Others of us like to listen to familiar songs again and again.

Perhaps influencing and bringing out the best in others is about hearing the tune, realising the strength of an instrument, knowing when to conduct and let go, choosing to improvise or play a solo, getting in sync or tapping the right beat and even giving applause.

But really when it comes down to it, music (like a person), is there to be enjoyed and mostly to be heard. If we listen deeply enough we just might catch a glimpse of the soul, the purest note or melody that emanates from the source of the instrument or the symphony and this might in turn evoke a more intimate and soulful melody in ourselves, ultimately helping us to realise that we are all parts from the same symphony.

Appendix

64 ways to build positive influence

∞

Values: Take time to explore and identify what your most important values are. Once you have done this, set small manageable goals to prioritise them.

∞

Intentions: Get clear in your mind what your intentions are for yourself and what your intentions are in relation to others. When attempting to influence others be clear about your true intentions and be willing to make them transparent.

∞

Loyalty and honour: Protect the honour of others when they are not around, even those you do not like. Tap into your own sense of honour.

Promises and commitments: Only make promises you will keep and keep them. If you break promises or don't follow through remember to apologise and also remember that the apology will not always necessarily set things straight but it is a beginning.

∞

Competence: Look for ways of realistically assess your competence so as to establish what you need to improve on. Try to do one thing each day to improve your competence. Avoid trying to appear more competent than you truly are.

∞

Congruence: Work at being true to yourself while cultivating genuine compassion for others. Try to avoid protecting yourself and others behind a façade of caretaking. Walk your talk, avoid saying things you don't really mean and follow through on commitments. Pay closer attention to your feelings and needs and check to see if your communication is in contradiction with what you are really feeling. People who pick up on this will see it as duplicitous.

∞

Confidence: Turn down the volume of your inner critic except where it genuinely serves you in being at your best. Build a strong confident image of yourself being at your best. Regularly take time out to affirm your strengths and achievements. Remind yourself that it is your own approval you need more than that of others.

∞

Root confidence: Write a mission/purpose statement that can guide you in any situation and speaks to you at your core. Begin to breathe deeper and acknowledge and affirm yourself a little more often. Recognise the fact that your inner confidence is exactly that, "inner". Let go of the need for other people to affirm you or build your confidence.

Empathy: Practice for small amounts of time (10 minutes a day is a good start) working at understanding the needs, emotions and viewpoints of others. Be sure your intention is to genuinely understand the other and don't do it with the intention of getting them to reciprocate or understand you better – this usually leads to resentment. Empathy is an act of giving not taking. Test your understanding by stating what you think they mean or reflecting their feeling state.

∞

Value differences: Practice valuing when others show difference of opinion. Observe or notice when you find this difficult or when you resist accepting others' difference. Ask yourself what unconscious needs or drives might be blocking you from accepting the other person as they are.

∞

Refine your communication: Pick a day to practice refinement when expressing opinions; qualify your generalisations. For example, instead of "it's great" or "it's awful" use "I like" or "I dislike". Cut out making gross judgements and generalisations about people, "she is just……", he is an awful………..". These kinds of communication significantly lower your credibility.

∞

Speaking: When speaking, ask yourself if you can see from the perspective of the other person and whether you need to adapt accordingly. Ask yourself who is doing most of the talking and whether you are dominating and need to move over to listening a little more.

∞

Align your communication with your intentions and expectations. If you have an expectation or an intention that you haven't expressed clearly it is unfair to expect others to read your mind and particularly unfair to punish them for an "offense" they were not aware of committing. In the law ignorance is no defence but in relationships it often is.

∞

Listening to understand: Try to gain an understanding of when and why it is hard for you to listen when interacting with others. Tune into what feelings or needs might be underneath the surface and see if you can transcend them in the moment or if you can discuss them with the person.

∞

Building others: Work at seeing the potential in others. Give more praise (or even some praise). Take the time to understand what motivates others positively, what they like, what they are passionate about. Give of your time and attention where you might not normally. Try to push yourself to cultivate interest when you typically cut off or your mind wanders.

Reducing others: Raise awareness of the times when you might reduce others by lowering their sense of self-worth, refusing to respond to their bids for your attention.

∞

5:1 ratio: Become aware of the incidental reactions you give to others. Try to increase the amount of positive attention you give and feelings you express particularly with people you love and care about but also with those with whom you need to build a positive relationship.

∞

Feel the fear and seek feedback: Genuinely ask people for feedback, "how do you think I am doing in relation to………..?" Be willing to accept the feedback and don't make any excuses or explanations when you receive it, instead ask for more specific insights so that you can understand how they are perceiving you.

The person and the behaviour: Separate people from their behaviour and their problems. See people as more than their current behaviour and strictly avoid using the behaviour to describe the person, as in, "this is just typical of them and the way they go on, they are so selfish."

∞

Nurture the seeds of growth in the beginner. With people who are young, innocent or starting out at something you have experience of, be careful not to infect them with your cynicism and give them lots of encouragement.

Beginner's mind-set: Try to have a beginner's mind-set while acknowledging your own competence. Use your competence effectively but avoid blowing your own trumpet.

∞

Role model: Ask yourself how your role model or someone you respect and admire would respond in your situation. Ask yourself how you can be a role model in a difficult interaction or with a person you find difficult.

∞

Positive bias: Tint your glasses a little to the positive when seeing others. It is unrealistic but so is the other bias and most people would prefer you to see them in a positive light.

∞

Look up: Look up to all people as being more experienced in <u>their world</u> than you are. Catch yourself being condescending, prejudiced, biased, snobby, arrogant, expert and grand standing and have a good laugh at your little ego looking for a little light.

∞

Stop bitching, whining, moaning and giving out about things you are unwilling or unable to try and change. Instead try choosing to talk about what is working or what is right with other people and their efforts to make the best of their life.

∞

Take the first step: When relationships breakdown be the one who takes the initiative to make reparations. Stop expecting others to be the one because they owe it to you or because you think it is always you that has to do it. If you want to build a relationship with someone you have to take responsibility for the building.

∞

Own up to your mistakes, errors, offenses and don't make needless excuses for them and lengthy explanations for them.

Allow yourself to be influenced by others from time to time especially those you think you are "better than" or "more intelligent" than or "more mature" than.

∞

Treat me like I'm cool: Treat the person talking to you as if they are the most important person in the world. Most, if not all people, want to be treated like they matter and it is not a difficult thing to treat them like they do.

∞

One extra action: Do one extra action at the end of each day that will impact positively on others. Don't fall into the trap of wanting a return for this.

∞

Give a break: See others as people who are doing their best given their current context and stage of development (this applies particularly to children and parents).

Choose when to tell, sell or involve. Involving others is usually their preference but sometimes you need to tell or instruct and sometimes you need to convince or sell through sound logic and/or evidence.

∞

Before reacting to negative stuff – S.T.O.P.

Still yourself.

Take at least three deep breaths.

Open yourself to options and possibilities.

Proceed with purpose.

∞

Mentoring moments: Be aware of mentoring moments when you can be a guiding light for others. Ask yourself how you can set the example or be a role model a little more often.

∞

When to lead when to follow: Choose when to lead and when to take a back seat. Giving other people the opportunity to lead and becoming a trusting follower yourself can be a powerful way of showing your trust in them.

∞

Area of influence: Believe that you have more power to influence than you currently know. Try to choose specific areas in which to focus your influence.

∞

A rock of strength: Work at being a rock of strength when people are in turmoil. Have the courage to face their fears with them, realise your desire to escape from the pain of others and make attempts to rise above that desire and stay the course.

∞

Manage the fixer in you: Avoid giving people *your* quick solutions to *their* problems when often all they really need is for you to be there to listen and empathize.

∞

Cultivate compassion: Occasionally practice being a compassionate, calm presence when with others. Meditate on the suffering and challenges of others. Mentally extend a sense of compassion and warmth to them.

∞

Choose the adult: Become aware of when the inner child in you is rebelling or conforming by default and work at choosing a more adult response.

∞

Mind your cynic: Notice when your cynical self emerges and tune into what is underneath the cynicism, it is often fear, resentment or anger. Realise that your expressed cynicism usually has a negative effect.

∞

Contain the negative: Realise the impact your negative moods can have on others and work at containing them or rising above them and choosing more skillful methods.

∞

Stop looking for other people or the world to be nice, caring, generous to you as if it is owed to you. Instead choose to be nice, caring, generous to others or the world from time to time.

∞

Stand up for what is right: Take a stance on injustice, inequality, prejudice, oppression. Be a courageous voice for those who may not always be able to find theirs.

∞

Set clear personal boundaries. Be responsible for your own thoughts, feelings and actions. Know what you like and dislike, what you will do and will not do and what you want and need. Be willing to ask for your needs to be met while accepting the right of others to refuse to meet your needs.

∞

Respect others' boundaries: This is going to seem a bit negative but it's as much instruction to myself as anyone else. Turn up on time and don't blame anyone but yourself when you don't. Don't out-stay your welcome. Don't blame others for how you feel. Don't act as if others' feelings are your responsibility. Don't push your opinions on others. The list here could be exhausting.

∞

Empower yourself: Realise that most of your personal power comes from within. In trying situations ask yourself whether you are giving away personal power. If certain types of behaviour in others always gives rise to negative reactions in you it is usually a sign that you are allowing them to have power over you. Try using the STOP acronym above and asking yourself whether you can choose to consciously let them have the power or consciously to retain your power.

∞

Empower others: Be willing to let others take the lead or be in charge on occasions. Always try to act as if healthy people have the power to take care of themselves while at the same time showing compassionate understanding for their set of circumstances.

∞

Give your focused attention. Focus on one conversation at a time, including the conversation in your head.

∞

Build collaboration and community: Find a way that you can contribute to collaboration and community. This could be in or out of work but it is likely to require your physical presence – rather than your digital or financial presence.

∞

Empathy is more an attitude than a technique, without the attitude of understanding, the techniques of empathic listening are often seen as empty and superficial. Work on developing an attitude of genuinely trying to understand the other.

∞

Make regular investments in trust with people you need to influence.

∞

Never presume that you have really understood another person's world. There is usually a lot more than you know going on.

Instead ask yourself if you can listen and understand them a little more deeply than you currently do.

∞

Raise your awareness of your own ego. Don't be fooled into thinking you don't have one, everyone does and we would be lost without it. However, most of our egos can be vulnerable and a bit toxic to others. Start becoming aware of when yours might be having a negative impact.

∞

Feedback: Give honest sincere feedback but keep in mind that it is not always necessary, will not always be heeded and you need to let go afterwards.

∞

See strengths: Acknowledge the strengths in others. Be willing to see the positive qualities in people. If you cannot see them and you genuinely want to build a positive relationship take the time to observe and see them in a way you never have before. If you are a manager I recommend keeping a database of your team member's strengths.

∞

Build on strengths: Where you can give people an opportunity to use and optimise their strengths. Give people what they need to succeed and praise their efforts.

∞

Open to growth: Demonstrate a willingness to grow and explore new avenues. Open your eyes, your heart and your mind to new ways of allowing your positive influence to flourish.

∞

Try on the cloak of humility. Accept your vulnerabilities and let go of self-righteousness. Most people prefer this to arrogance.

∞

Accept your negative impact: Acknowledge the fact that you can have a negative impact on others and regardless of what happens, in some cases, you may not be able to change that fact.

∞

Learn from crisis: Work at seeing the learning from crisis sooner than you might ordinarily do.

∞

Good enough: Know when good enough is good enough. Let go of the need for things to be perfect. We live in a perfectly imperfect world. The sooner we can learn to let go of our need for control and perfection the sooner we might find some inner calm which we may then start communicating outward.

∞

Stubbornness: When feeling stubborn for no other reason than it is your default or your ego is in a panic, try to soften your attitude and see what happens. A few deep breaths and a bit of empathy is usually a good start.

∞

Forgiveness: Work at forgiving people a little sooner and a little more often. Most of the offenses people commit in relationships are not big things and are done unintentionally and without any malice at all. In fact, often that person believed they were acting with good intentions. If we can see this we realise that it is something else that is stopping us from forgiving – maybe there is even someone else we need to forgive not the person with whom we are currently angry. Even when acts are significant and done intentionally at some point we may need to forgive in order to let go and move on.

∞

Be compassionate with yourself: Allow yourself to be the unique, perfect yet flawed human being that you are. See yourself as a person in a state of becoming. Give yourself a break and nurture the seeds of love, courage, compassion, wisdom and positive influence that are there within you.

∞

ABOUT THE AUTHOR

Peter Connolly is a coaching psychologist who has worked with a large number of individuals and organisations in Ireland and across Europe. He has worked as a facilitator with Franklin Covey, a Leadership Specialist with Intel and currently teaches as an associate with the Irish Management Institute. He also runs two businesses, Peter Connolly Associates which specializes in Management/Leadership development and Learning Cogs which specializes in the design of soft-skills training as well as training simulations and exercises. Peter has been married for 24 years and has two children.